THE HERITAGE OF

SOUTHERN COOKING

ISBN 1-57912-263-9

Library of Congress Cataloging-in-Publication Data on file at Black Dog & Leventhal Publishers, Inc. Available upon request.

Cover and interior design: 27.12 Design Ltd. (www.2712design.com)

Art direction and prop styling: 27.12 Design Ltd.

Photography: Michael Cogliantry (michaelcogliantry.com)

Food styling: Tracy Harlor

Special thanks for editorial services to Carol Anderson, Lindley Boegehold, Anne Burns, Sara Cameron, and Dara Lazar.

Additional thanks to Kevin Klenner at Kuttner Prop Rentals, Elias Mayeri of Red's Antiques & Rugs, John Derrick at the Christopher Street Flea Market,
Irene 'Mike' Michels, Greta Niles, Constance Nadig, Abigail Chipley, Meredith Regas, Skye Fraser, Norman and Esther Harte, and Martin Hossfeld.

Manufactured in Spain

Published by

Black Dog & Leventhal Publishers, Inc.

151 West 19th Street

New York, New York 10011

Distributed by

Workman Publishing Company

708 Broadway

New York, New York 10003

g f e d c b a

THE HERITAGE OF
SOUTHERN COOKING

An Inspired Tour of Southern Cuisine Including Regional Specialties,
Heirloom Favorites, and Original Dishes

Camille Glenn

Black Dog
& Leventhal
Publishers
New York

CONTENTS

MY HERITAGE OF SOUTHERN COOKING

It has for many years been my belief that most of us have a soft spot in our hearts for the foods that we grew up on, especially if that food was delicious. In the case of some memoirs and biographies I have read, the food was not really good but still it evoked memories, pleasant or otherwise. Such was the case of Marcel Proust, the French novelist, writing about his Aunt Léonie's stale madeleines—so stale that she had to dip them in her cup of hot tea to soften them, but the taste evoked a memory Proust recalled with love.

The exchange of letters between Thomas Jefferson and Mary Randolph, his daughter in Virginia, makes luscious reading. Not only did they write about new ideas and recipes in detail but they delineated their concerns about the garden, the orchard, and the vineyard Jefferson planned for Monticello. Even well into old age, Jefferson's writings are filled with memories of good food he had eaten in Europe as our ambassador, in the White House, as well as in Virginia. He was the quintessential gourmet.

Taste memory is a very real thing, and it seems to vary greatly in people. Those who have a deep interest in wonderful food and cooking seem to have the most reliable taste memory.

I was reared in a Southern family so "food-minded" that we talked about good food all the time. Many times while we were eating a delicious meal at the family table we would be reminded of and discuss other dishes that would have been good too, and would recall memorable meals that we had had in foreign countries, in restaurants, or at home.

My parents had a little hotel in Dawson Springs, Kentucky, a so-called health resort or spa. Mother supervised the kitchen and dining room and most every day took a hand in the cooking, she loved it so. I shall never forget her noodle board filled with drying noodles, to be served with Kentucky shoulder of veal roast. It was truly milk-fed veal, almost white and oh, so tender. They had to cook several of these roasts at a time for the hotel, and that was the richest and best gravy on earth—a light golden brown, and so very lightly thickened with flour one would never suspect it was there at all.

I can remember so well the bobwhite quail we had in the winter, sautéed to a perfect glistening brown and served always with hot biscuits and cream gravy. Oh, to taste that quail once more—it was moist and crunchy and beautiful. I think I do taste it—the picture is so clear in my mind it is almost like being there again in that large dining room with the family table in a corner. When Mother cooked something special for us, like the crappie and bass Daddy had caught in Reelfoot Lake in Tennessee, we had to wait until the guests were gone.

Devil's Rock in Tradewater River, not far from our little town, was a good place to fish when the crappie were biting in the spring. Never shall I forget the day when I, a tiny thirteen-year-old, caught a 1½-pound crappie—and my scream was heard all the way to the old mill. Dozens of fishermen hurried to the rescue. Sorry, folks, my brother said, Camille just caught a fish, that's all. I guess that scream is still in the airwaves around Devil's Rock, and the flavor of that crappie, which Mother cooked that night, will never leave me.

We had the food of the season back then, and we cannot improve upon that now. The changing seasons are our best guides still. When the snow was on the ground and the cold air had made us as hungry as all get-out, we would have Hunter's Veal Stew, and it would soothe our tummies and warm our bones. You couldn't improve on that today. Have this stew next winter, with a warm pudding or Windfall Apple Pie for dessert. Never a frivolous dessert after a hearty meal—the counterpoint of dishes must blend.

The June peas and new potatoes will soon be in, and they are worth waiting for. Do have them with lamb or veal. For a glorious occasion, have Watermelon and Raspberry Sherbet or the Golden Cointreau Cake, the most special cake in this book. The Cointreau Cake seems at its best with strawberries or pineapple, chilled or in sherbet. Ice cream is too rich.

Over the years I have cooked every recipe in this book, and hundreds more. I believe that delicious food is an essential part of the good life, and that the hours spent in the kitchen is time well spent, and fun.

Build a repertoire of the menus you like best for your family and for parties. Cook the dishes over and over again. Memorize them—make them a part of you. Then you will be at ease with company and can reap the joy of the kitchen.

—Camille Glenn
Louisville, Kentucky

BEAUTIFUL BEGINNINGS

The charm of appetizers and hors d'oeuvres is not only their delicious flavors but also their versatility. Because of the longer summer days in the South, they serve us well for patio parties, outdoor grilling, or for light luncheon dishes. With a touch of improvisation they make exquisite first courses served at the table in any season. Not every appetizer or hors d'oeuvre fills the entire bill, but as you work with them you will find they are flexible indeed, and in many cases they make superb garnishes for important dishes.

The Sarapico Stuffed Shrimp, for instance, is a delectable "pick-up" appetizer for cocktail parties, but served on Boston or Bibb lettuce with a wedge or two of tomato and several huge black olives, it also makes an exquisite luncheon salad or first course.

Crackers are often perfect accompaniments to serve with appetizers, but they must be bland and crisp. Their function is to lend texture and to blend, not disturb, the flavors of the appetizers. Crackers that contain malt, powdered garlic or onion, or garlic salt are not suitable.

PERNOD

The Pernod can of course be omitted, but it gives the authentic flavor. Licorice-tasting absinthe was the original liqueur used in these oysters, but it was declared against the law in the U.S. years ago, as the wormwood in the true absinthe and its high alcoholic strength—136 percent—are said to cause deterioration of the brain. Pernod from France (where absinthe is also prohibited) has a definite licorice flavor but is only 80 percent proof, and there's no wormwood. Fennel and tarragon have a slight licorice taste also, but fennel is the more assertive.

OYSTERS ROCKEFELLER

[SERVES 6]

In looking through my files I found a very old letter from Antoine's restaurant in New Orleans that was written in answer to my inquiry about the true origin of Oysters Rockefeller. The letter was from a descendant of Jules Alciatore, verifying that Jules, the original owner of Antoine's, had indeed created Oysters Rockefeller in 1899. The recipe was not given. Legend had insisted that on his deathbed Alciatore exacted a promise that no one would reveal the exact proportions of the recipe. It has been told, too, that when Alciatore first originated the famous oyster dish, he commented that it was as rich as Rockefeller, and the name stuck.

It is believed that watercress was used first instead of spinach, and it is rather certain that there was a dash of absinthe—how much, we do not know. All through the years, this has remained a classic and favorite way of preparing oysters, which is the greatest test of all—the test of time.

24	oysters on the half-shell (shucked and loosened; see box, page 8)
6	cups rock salt
1	cup (2 sticks) unsalted butter, at room temperature
$^1/_3$	cup water
$^1/_3$	cup minced shallots or scallions (green onions)
2	cups packed watercress or spinach leaves
$^2/_3$	cup finely chopped fresh parsley
$^2/_3$	cup finely chopped fresh tarragon
	Salt and freshly ground black pepper to taste
	Cayenne pepper to taste
$^1/_4$	cup chopped fennel, if available
4	teaspoons Pernod

1. Place the oysters in their shells on a bed of rock salt (about $1^1/_2$ inches deep) in one or more baking pans. Set aside. (The rock salt keeps the oysters upright and holds the heat while they are cooking.)
2. Preheat the oven to 450°F.
3. Combine 4 tablespoons of the butter with the water and shallots or scallions in a saucepan and simmer until they are limp and the water has boiled away, about 5 minutes. The shallots must not brown or sizzle the least bit. Add the watercress or spinach, parsley, and tarragon. Heat only until the watercress has wilted, just a few seconds. It must not actually cook. Add the salt, pepper, and cayenne.
4. Purée the watercress mixture with the fennel, Pernod, and remaining butter in a food processor until it is perfectly smooth, less than a minute. Put a spoonful of the mixture on top of each oyster.
5. Bake the oysters on the middle shelf of the oven until the sauce is bubbly hot, about 5 minutes. They must not overcook.

OYSTERS ON THE HALF-SHELL

[SERVES 6]

Buy oysters in shells that are tightly closed. This indicates freshness, and that's what you want.

18 to 36 oysters (depending on size)
Mignonette Sauce or Caviar Garnish (recipes follow)

Scrub the unopened oyster shells thoroughly with a stiff brush under running water. Shuck the oysters (see sidebar) and drain them. Place the oysters, in their shells, on a bed of crushed ice and add your choice of garnish.

MIGNONETTE SAUCE

1   cup tarragon vinegar
¼   cup finely chopped shallots, or more to taste
     Salt and freshly ground white or black pepper to taste
     Lemon wedges

1.   Combine the vinegar, shallots, salt, and pepper. Stir well.
2.   Garnish the oysters with lemon wedges and serve with a sauceboat of Mignonette Sauce.

•   There should be a generous amount of pepper—white is traditional, but whichever you use, it must be freshly ground. If you can't find shallots, wait until you can. Onions won't do.

CAVIAR GARNISH

3 to 6 tablespoons black caviar
18 to 36 thin half-slices lemon (2 lemons)
Watercress or parsley sprigs

Place ½ teaspoon caviar on top of each oyster and then add a lemon slice. Garnish the ice between the shells with watercress or parsley.

HOW TO SHUCK AN OYSTER

A strong oyster knife is imperative. Hold the oyster with the hinge part of the shell in the palm of your hand. Push the blade of a thick oyster knife between the two shells near the hinge and run it around between the shells until you cut the muscle that holds the upper and lower valves together. The lid should pop open.

When the lid pops open, lift up the top shell and sever the muscle attached to it with the point of a sharp paring knife. The liquor around oysters that have been shucked must be clear and the odor pleasing. A bad oyster is easy to detect by its unpleasant odor and milky liquor.

TOAST CHARLOTTE

This is a delectable way of serving a crisp, warm toast. It is the low temperature that does the trick. At 325°F the bread toasts from the inside out—and it stays crisp a long time.

Use white homemade-type bread sliced thin. Cut each piece in half. Lay the pieces on a baking sheet. Brush the tops lightly with melted butter, covering the entire surface. Sprinkle with poppy seeds, if desired. Bake in a pre-heated 325°F oven until golden brown, about 25–30 minutes. Serve warm with cheese, pates, soups, and salads.

SMOKED BACON TWIRLS WITH ROSEMARY

[SERVES 4 TO 6]

Meals in the dining car of the old Illinois Central Railroad, which ran from Chicago to New Orleans in the early decades of the twentieth century, may not have been as glamorous as dining on the Orient Express, but it was high adventure for us. The delicious food that came from that postage-stamp-size kitchen was amazing. We dined on the delicacies of the South—oysters, shrimp, and strawberries in season. For breakfast there were omelets, grits, country ham, hot biscuits, and bacon twirls galore with silver pots of freshly brewed coffee. The bacon twirls were very special. The Henry Mobley family in Mississippi employed a retired Pullman chef as their cook for a while, and this is the way he said the twirls were done.

1   pound finest smoked bacon, sliced

1½ tablespoons crushed dried rosemary

1. Preheat the oven to 400°F.
2. Place the bacon slices on a baking sheet. Bake until the bacon is only half done, about 8 minutes. Remove, and sprinkle ¼ teaspoon rosemary on each slice.
3. Allow the bacon to cool slightly, then roll each piece in a tight twirl and spear it with a toothpick to hold it together.
4. When almost ready to serve, preheat the oven again to 400°F. Place the bacon back on the baking sheet and bake until thoroughly done but not overly crisp, about 8 minutes. (If you use thick-sliced bacon, allow 20 minutes, or more, total cooking time.)
5. Serve as hors d'oeuvres, or with scrambled eggs or an omelet for breakfast on a special day.

VARIATION

- The bacon twirls (minus toothpicks) may be served on top of a green salad. Divine.

SARAPICO STUFFED SHRIMP

[SERVES 4 TO 6]

These shrimp are as delicious as they are versatile: They can be served on ice as a buffet hors d'oeuvre, they are charming served on a bed of Bibb lettuce and watercress as a first course, and they can also be a luncheon dish. Shrimp and Roquefort blend exquisitely. The amount of stuffing needed will vary with the size of the shrimp.

12	jumbo or large shrimp
3	ounces Roquefort or blue cheese
3	ounces cream cheese
	Salt to taste
	Cayenne pepper to taste
$^2/_3$	cup minced fresh parsley
	Watercress or parsley sprigs, for garnish
$1^1/_2$	cups large black olives
6	slivers red bell or pimiento pepper

1. Cook the shrimp in a large pot of boiling salted water, or in water seasoned with Shrimp or Crab Boil (see sidebar), until pink, 2 to 4 minutes. Drain the shrimp and allow them to cool slightly.

2. Shell the shrimp, but leave the tails intact. Remove the black vein. Cut the shrimp almost all the way through along the length, making a pocket for stuffing.

3. Blend the Roquefort or blue cheese and the cream cheese in a food processor or with an electric mixer. Add salt and cayenne pepper to taste. Stuff a small amount of the cheese mixture into the cavity of each shrimp. (Jumbo shrimp will take about 1 scant tablespoon; large shrimp, about 2 teaspoons.) Dip the stuffed side of the shrimp into the minced parsley.

4. For a cocktail party, serve on a large bed of crushed ice garnished with watercress or parsley, with a mound of huge black olives in the center of a platter. Scatter the slivers of red bell pepper or pimiento over the platter. Very beautiful.

• The shrimp can be stuffed several hours ahead. Cover with plastic wrap and refrigerate until ready to serve.

VARIATIONS

• The Roquefort and cream cheese can be thinned with cream or milk (cream is best) and used as a dip for the shrimp. Fresh dill is a delicious addition to the dip.

• As a first course or for a luncheon: Place the stuffed shrimp on a salad plate lined with watercress or Bibb lettuce. (Allow 3 jumbo or 4 to 5 large shrimp per serving.) Sprinkle each shrimp with $^1/_2$ teaspoon Classic Vinaigrette (see page 61) Garnish each plate with 2 black olives and a sliver of red bell pepper or pimiento. Serve with hot buttered crackers.

SHRIMP OR CRAB BOIL

[MAKES $^2/_3$ CUP]

Imported bay leaves should be used in this mixture. For each pound of shrimp or blue crab, use 3 tablespoons of seasoning, plus 2 slices lemon, to 1 quart of cold water.

$^1/_4$ cup coriander seeds

$^1/_2$ cup yellow mustard seeds

1 dried red pepper, crushed (about 1 tablespoon)

2 imported bay leaves, crumbled

3 whole cloves

8 whole allspice

$1^1/_4$ tablespoons coarse (kosher) salt

1. Combine all the ingredients and mix well. If stored in a tightly covered, clean jar in a cool, dry place, it will keep for 6 months. 2. To use, tie the seasoning mixture in a cheesecloth bag. Drop it into the water in a stainless-steel or enamel saucepan along with the lemon slices, bring to a boil, and simmer 10 minutes. 3. Add the shrimp (in their shells) or hard-shell crabs and boil gently, uncovered, 1 to 3 minutes for shrimp (depending upon the size), 20 minutes for crabs. 4. Drain and use as directed.

VERY SPECIAL CHEESE STRAWS

[MAKES 90 STRAWS]

1   pound aged sharp Cheddar cheese
8   tablespoons (1 stick) unsalted butter
1   teaspoon cayenne pepper
1/2 teaspoon salt
2   cups sifted all-purpose flour

1. Grate the cheese by hand or in a food processor. Cut the butter into pieces and blend it with the cheese, in the processor or with an electric mixer, until smooth. Add the cayenne pepper, salt, and flour. Mix well. 2. Chill the dough for at least 1 hour, so it will be easier to handle. 3. You can prepare the straws with a cookie press, using the thin serrated ribbon blade to create 3-inch straws. Or you can form the dough into small balls, then roll them into thin rounds. Use the tines of a fork to etch grooves into the rounds. 4. Preheat the oven to 325°F. 5. Lay the straws on a lightly greased baking sheet and bake until done, about 30 minutes. The straws should have a slight tinge of brown on the bottom, but not on the top. If they brown too much, they will toughen.

OLD KENTUCKY BEER CHEESE
[SERVES 15 TO 20]

In the early days of the twentieth century there was a German saloon keeper in Frankfort (Kentucky's state capital) who created this cheese and kept large crocks of it on the counter of his saloon. A nickel glass of beer entitled a customer to ham sandwiches, pickled oysters, potato salad, and cracker after cracker spread with beer cheese—and the saloon keeper was solvent! Anyway, this German beer cheese is still the very best. You must, of course, start with an excellent cheese—as the saloon keeper did.

2   pounds sharp Cheddar cheese, at room temperature
2   cloves garlic, mashed
3   tablespoons Worcestershire sauce
1   teaspoon dry mustard
    Tabasco sauce to taste
1/2 bottle beer, or more as necessary
1   teaspoon salt, or to taste

1. Cut the cheese into cubes and place them in a food processor or an electric mixer. Process until perfectly smooth. Add the garlic, Worcestershire, mustard, and Tabasco. Blend well.
2. Add the beer, a little at a time, while continuing to beat the cheese, until the mixture is a good, firm, spreading consistency. (Too much beer will make the cheese too fluffy.) Stir in the salt and refrigerate. (This is a superb keeper.)
3. Serve on small slices of rye or pumpernickel bread, or on crackers. Delicious with cold, cold beer.

WASHINGTON WATERFRONT PICKLED SHRIMP
[SERVES 4 TO 6]

When we lived in Washington, D.C., before and during World War II, huge glass vats of pickled shrimp lined the walls of the seafood shops on the waterfront. They were plentiful, cheap, and made a glorious snack or hors d'oeuvre. That picturesque sight has vanished—pickled shrimp are no longer plentiful, nor are they cheap, but they are still glorious.

1^1/$_2$	cups distilled white vinegar
^{1}/$_2$	cup water
3	tablespoons coriander seeds
2	teaspoons mustard seeds
^{1}/$_4$	teaspoon dry mustard
1 or 2	blades mace
1	large piece dried ginger
	Salt to taste
3	cups cooked medium shrimp, shelled and deveined
^{1}/$_2$	cup thinly sliced mild onion
1	lemon, thinly sliced and seeded
1	tiny piece red chile pepper
2	bay leaves

1. Combine the vinegar, water, coriander seeds, mustard seeds, dry mustard, mace, and ginger in a stainless-steel or enamel pan and cook at a medium boil for 10 minutes. Add salt to taste. Remove from the heat and allow to cool.

2. In a quart jar, pack the shrimp, onion, lemon, chile pepper, and bay leaves in layers. Pour in the marinade. Press the contents firmly in the jar until they are completely submerged.

3. Refrigerate for 36 hours. Turn the jar upside down a few times during the first 24 hours so the spices are distributed.

4. Serve ice cold on toothpicks as an hors d'oeuvre, or on a bed of chopped parsley as a first course.

HERB VINEGARS

Vinegars with an infusion of fresh herbs are easy to make, but many homemade concoctions are travesties of fine flavor. In the first place, the vinegar chosen must be fine enough to be used alone. White distilled vinegar is for pickling, not for salads. Malt vinegar has no place in a good kitchen.

Tarragon vinegar is a star. It is an essential in a great kitchen. It speaks up, so do not use it where the tarragon flavor is not compatible.

Parsley, dill, rosemary, mint, and sweet basil (not purple basil, please) are the other herbs that make fair vinegars. They are made exactly like tarragon vinegar.

THE SONG OF THE SOUP KETTLE

Delicious homemade soups have the culinary grace of being adaptable to everyone's taste and pocketbook. Soup can be a meal in itself, thick and hearty for a cold winter night or well chilled with a sprinkling of fresh herbs for a hot summer day. Or at least that's the way we've always enjoyed it in the South. Few dishes give us a greater feeling of well-being than a good soup. Few dishes are a greater challenge to the cook than a good soup, with the possible exception of homemade bread. And the two are soul mates.

If the stock is made of chicken, veal, or beef, it must be well seasoned with vegetables and herbs until it is delicious all on its own.

If it is to be a cream soup with character and flavor, whole milk with a judicious amount of heavy cream must be used. Skimmed and 2 percent milk are for diets, not for wonderful soups. They will curdle when boiled and are flavorless to begin with. Cream has flavor. Cooks find that so-called half-and-half, which is seldom half cream and half milk, as it is reputed to be, also curdles when boiled. Heavy cream when fresh will boil down and thicken without curdling—a good cook's technique for making delicious soups and sauces without the heavy, flour-thickened roux of the old cuisine.

QUICK TOMATO CONSOMMÉ

[SERVES 4]

An easy cup of warming soup for a wintry night.

1 can (10¹/₂ ounces) undiluted beef consommé
1 cup water
2 cups tomato juice
1 bay leaf
1 rib celery
3 slices sweet white onion
3 springs parsley
  Salt to taste
  Chopped fresh parsley, for garnish
4 thin lemon slices, for garnish

Combine all the ingredients except the chopped parsley and lemon in a saucepan. Bring to a boil, reduce the heat, and simmer for 15 – 18 minutes. Strain. Serve with a sprinkling of parsley and a slice of lemon.

Unless I specifically mention it, do not cover your soup pot. A cover causes the vegetables to steam and become mushy.

BEEF, TOMATO & OKRA SOUP

[SERVES 6]

This typical Creole soup is not supposed to be thick and hearty with an overabundance of vegetables, but very flavorful and thinning!

3 pounds beef short ribs
2 quarts cold water
  Bouquet garni of 2 bay leaves, several sprigs parsley, and a generous pinch of dried thyme, tied in a cheesecloth bag
2 medium onions, peeled and left whole
2 carrots, cut in half
¹/₄ pound small tender string beans
4 ribs celery, chopped
3 large ripe tomatoes, peeled, seeded, and chopped; or canned whole tomatoes, drained and chopped
¹/₂ large green bell pepper, cored, seeded, and cut into slivers
³/₄ pound fresh okra, thickly sliced
¹/₃ cup raw rice or small pasta
  Salt and freshly ground black pepper to taste
¹/₃ cup chopped fresh parsley
  Bouquet of mixed fresh herbs, such as basil, chervil, marjoram, and tarragon

1. Put the meat in a soup kettle or large Dutch oven. Add the water and bring to a boil. After boiling 5 or 6 minutes, begin to skim off any scum that rises. Skim often to keep the stock clear.

2. Add the bouquet garni, onions, and carrots. Continue to simmer, uncovered, until the meat is tender, 1 to 1¹/₂ hours.

3. Add the beans, celery, tomatoes, and bell pepper. Continue to cook for 25 to 30 minutes.

4. Lift out the meat and set it aside. Discard the bouquet garni, carrots, and onions. Add the okra and rice or pasta and cook until done, about 20 minutes. Season with salt and pepper.

5. Five minutes before serving, toss in the chopped parsley and a fresh herb bouquet if available. Serve with slices of the meat, mustard, and French bread—or with thin cucumber sandwiches.

NORTH CAROLINA CHICKEN, RICE & CABBAGE SOUP

[SERVES 6]

Cabbage of any type should be blanched for 2 minutes in boiling water, then drained well before it is added to soup. This is the expert way of handling strong-flavored vegetables in soups and stews. In the fall, ripe red bell peppers are a beautiful addition to this soup.

6	cups Rich Chicken Stock (see sidebar)
2	medium onions, sliced
$1/2$	cup rice
$1/2$	large head green cabbage, torn into medium-size pieces
2	lemon slices
$1/2$	pound skinless, boneless chicken, freshly cooked and slivered
3	tablespoons chopped fresh parsley
	Salt and freshly ground white pepper to taste
	Cayenne pepper to taste

1. Put the chicken stock in a large saucepan. Bring to a boil, then add the onions and rice. Reduce the heat and simmer gently, uncovered, until the rice is almost tender, 15 to 20 minutes.

2. In the meantime, boil the cabbage for 2 minutes. Drain. Add the cabbage and lemon slices to the soup. Simmer for 5 to 7 minutes. (The cabbage must not lose its color.)

3. Add the chicken, parsley, and salt, pepper, and cayenne to taste. Simmer until the chicken is heated through. Serve with corn muffins or your favorite cornmeal bread.

RICH CHICKEN STOCK

Here is the expert way of giving this soup added flavor and color: Butter well half a chicken ($1^{1}/_{4}$ pounds). Place it in a preheated 450°F oven and bake until the chicken is a light golden brown, 20 minutes. Put the chicken in the stock and cook until tender and flavorful, 25 minutes. Remove the chicken from the stock. Allow it to cool, then skin, bone, and cut the meat into slivers. Proceed as directed.

SEASONING

Burgoo must be seasoned after it has been reduced in volume, or the seasonings will become too concentrated.

KENTUCKY BURGOO
[SERVES 10 - 15]

Kentucky Burgoo is a thick soup, not a stew. It is at its best in the late summer or early fall, when fresh vegetables are still available, but the goodness of the burgoo at any time depends on the judgment and talents of the cook.

1 or 2	beef or veal marrow bones, $2^{1}/_{2}$ to 3 pounds
2	pounds beef chuck or lean short ribs
2	pounds breast of lamb
2	pounds breast of veal
1	stewing hen, capon, or roasting chicken, 4 to 5 pounds
1	tender young rabbit, ready to cook
8	to 10 quarts water
2	onions, peeled
1	teaspoon dried thyme
2	bay leaves
4	ribs celery
6	sprigs parsley
$4^{1}/_{2}$	cups chopped onions (about $1^{1}/_{2}$ pounds)
$4^{1}/_{2}$	cups diced peeled potatoes (about $1^{1}/_{2}$ pounds)
4	carrots, peeled and diced
2	green bell peppers, cored, seeded, and slivered
2	red bell peppers, cored, seeded, and slivered
2	cups fresh lima beans
2	cups fresh corn kernels (4 to 6 ears)
2	cups chopped celery
$1^{1}/_{2}$	to 2 quarts canned tomatoes with their liquid, puréed
1	red chile pepper, or more to taste, sliced
	Salt to taste
$1^{1}/_{2}$	pounds small okra, carefully trimmed
	Freshly ground black pepper to taste
	Tabasco sauce to taste
	Worcestershire sauce to taste
1	cup chopped fresh parsley

1. Put marrow bones, beef, lamb, veal, fowl, and rabbit in a huge pot and cover with cold water. Bring slowly to a boil, then reduce the heat and allow the broth to simmer, skimming often. Add the onions, thyme, bay leaves, celery, and parsley sprigs.

2. Simmer, uncovered, removing the chicken and rabbit after 1 1/2 hours. Continue to cook until the remaining meat is tender enough to fall from the bones, an additional 3 to 4 hours. Cool.

3. Separate the meat, chicken, and rabbit from the bones. Cover and refrigerate. Strain the stock and refrigerate overnight to allow the fat to solidify.

4. The next day, remove most of the fat, but leave a little in the stock for flavor. Add the chopped onions, potatoes, carrots, bell peppers, lima beans, corn, celery, tomatoes, and chile pepper to the stock. Salt slightly. Bring to a boil, reduce the heat, and allow the soup to simmer very quietly, uncovered, until the vegetables are tender and the burgoo has cooked low, 1 to 2 hours. Add the okra with the meat during the last 30 to 40 minutes of cooking. Add water when necessary.

5. Season to taste with salt, freshly ground black pepper, Tabasco, and Worcestershire sauce. Stir in the chopped parsley. Serve with corn muffins or any good homemade bread and butter.

THYME

Thyme is the indispensable herb in most fine soup stocks. It has an intense flavor but is compatible with other herbs and is usable in a great variety of ways. It's the heart and soul of the bouquet garni. The New Orleans herb, as it is sometimes called, was brought to Louisiana by the French.

OYSTER & ARTICHOKE SOUP

[SERVES 4 TO 6]

The idea for this soup came to me from New Orleans. It is for the gourmet, and worth every effort it takes. The fresh artichokes can be tedious when a number are needed, so why not have a small gathering of your favorite "food-minded" friends and cook it together.

6	large artichokes, freshly cooked
4	tablespoons ($^1/_2$ stick) butter
6	shallots, minced
$^1/_3$	cup water
$2^1/_2$	tablespoons all-purpose flour
3	cups Veal or Chicken Stock (veal is best; see pages 38–39)
$^2/_3$	cup oyster liquor
2	bay leaves
3	sprigs fresh thyme or 1 teaspoon dried
	Salt and freshly ground white pepper to taste
	Cayenne pepper to taste
1	pint oysters
	Fresh lemon juice to taste
$^1/_4$	cup chopped fresh parsley
	Thin lemon slices, for garnish

1. Strip (and reserve) the flesh from the end of the artichoke leaves, scoop out the chokes, and cut the artichoke bottoms into cubes. You should have $1^1/_2$ to 2 cups of artichoke cubes and flesh.
2. Melt the butter in a medium saucepan and add the minced shallots. Add the water (so the shallots will cook without browning) and simmer until the shallots are tender.
3. When the water has boiled away, add the flour and blend it in. Add the stock, oyster liquor, bay leaves, and thyme. Sprinkle lightly with salt and white and cayenne peppers and allow the mixture to simmer about 5 minutes.
4. Stir in the oysters. Season with additional salt and white and cayenne peppers. Add lemon juice to taste. Stir in the parsley. Heat the soup until piping hot, just to the point where the oysters begin to curl. Garnish with lemon slices and serve at once in heated bouillon cups with French bread.

- If more liquid is needed, oyster liquor should be the first choice; if you don't have enough, use veal or chicken stock.

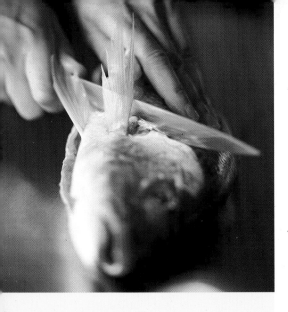

CHOWDER

The word "chowder" is believed to have come from the French word "chaudiere," the name of a large cauldron in which the fisherfolk of Brittany cooked their fish soups and stews.

In our country the earliest chowders came to us via the French and English colonizers. Potatoes were added somewhere along the way and today many chowders include them, except the Southern Seacoast gumbos, which are usually served with rice instead.

CAROLINA SILK SNAPPER CHOWDER

[SERVES 6 TO 8]

A large family of snappers swim from Cape Hatteras to Florida through the Bahamas. The silk snapper and the ever-popular red snapper are much alike in taste and texture.

5	cups Fish Stock (see page 38 and step 1) or Veal Stock (see page 39)
4	thick slices lean smoked bacon or salt pork
3	onions, peeled and cubed (2 cups)
1	pound Idaho potatoes, peeled and cubed (3 cups)
	Salt to taste
1	silk or red snapper, about 3 pounds, filleted and skinned
$1/3$	pound whole small shrimp, shelled (1 cup)
$1/2$	cup chopped red bell pepper
	Freshly ground white pepper to taste
$1/4$	teaspoon cayenne pepper, or more to taste
	Several slices fresh red chile pepper, or pinch dried hot red pepper (optional)
	Juice of $1/2$ lemon
	Chopped fresh parsley or chervil, for garnish

1. Make the fish stock following the directions for the basic Fish Stock (see page 38). Strain through dampened cheesecloth draped over a sieve. You may use the basic Veal Stock as is.
2. Sauté the bacon or salt pork in a heavy enamel or stainless-steel pot over medium heat, then lift it out and put it aside (if you used salt pork, discard it). Add the onions and potatoes to the pot. Strain the stock, through dampened cheesecloth or a fine sieve, over the vegetables. Add a touch of salt. Cook, uncovered, over medium-low heat until the onions and potatoes are tender, about 25 minutes.
3. Add the snapper fillets to the chowder and continue to simmer gently until the fish flakes with a fork, no more than 6 minutes. Add the shrimp and bell pepper and cook 2 to 3 minutes but no longer.
4. While it is cooking, season the chowder to taste with salt, white pepper, cayenne, and chile pepper. Add water if more liquid is needed. Break up the snapper a bit. The chowder must be thick but not so thick that one cannot eat it with a spoon. Add the lemon juice and sprinkle the chowder with parsley or chervil. Use the reserved bacon, crumbled, as a side dish for those who want it. Serve in soup plates with French bread or cornmeal muffins.

SPRING CONSOMME

This is a beautiful clear soup with an exquisite balance of flavors. Add only a tablespoon or so of vegetables to each serving. Just a touch of color in the crystal-clear broth is the most charming. Very small carrots may be scraped and scored deeply with a paring knife, then sliced crosswise very thin to look like daisies—beautiful.

Cut new turnips, carrots, and tiny green beans into little strips, not more than 1/2 inch long and toothpick thin. Add fresh young peas and cook the vegetables in boiling salted water until just tender, about 2 minutes. Drain and drop into hot consommé. Garnish with finely chopped chervil or parsley just before serving.

SHRIMP OR CRAWFISH BISQUE

[SERVES 6]

This shrimp or crawfish bisque is served at the most elegant homes in New Orleans and Charleston.

1	medium onion, chopped
3	carrots, peeled and chopped
4	ribs celery, chopped
1/2	cup finely chopped shallots or leeks
2	ripe tomatoes, peeled and puréed
3	tablespoons butter or good-quality olive oil
1/2	cup cold water
2	pounds small shrimp, or 10 pounds whole crawfish (for 2 pounds crawfish meat)
1	cup dry white wine
1	cup well-cooked rice, kept warm
4 – 5	cups Chicken, Veal, or Fish Stock (see pages 38–39)
	Salt and freshly ground white pepper to taste
1/2	teaspoon cayenne pepper
1	teaspoon Hungarian paprika
1	cup heavy or whipping cream
3	tablespoons unsalted butter

1. Combine the vegetables in a heavy enamel or stainless-steel pot. Add the butter or olive oil and the water and bring to a boil. Reduce the heat and simmer, stirring, until the vegetables are half-cooked, about 4 minutes. They must not be brown.
2. Add the shrimp or crawfish and toss them about until their shells turn a deep pink, 6 to 7 minutes.
3. Add the wine and simmer over low heat about 4 minutes.
4. Carefully lift out the seafood. Shell the shrimp or crawfish, reserving the meat.
5. Toss the shells into a wooden bowl and pound them with a mortar to break them into smaller pieces. Toss the shells back into the pot.
6. Add the warm rice and mix thoroughly.
7. Add 4 cups stock and stir until the mixture is the consistency of a very thick soup. Remove the pot from the heat, cover, and allow the flavors to ripen for 1 hour or more.
8. Put the mixture through a fine sieve. Add more stock if needed, but the soup must be thick. Season to taste with salt, white pepper, cayenne, and paprika. Place the bisque over low heat and add the cream and butter. Stir gently in one direction so the soup will thicken a bit.
9. If the shrimp seem too large, chop them into smaller pieces, then add them to the soup. If you are using crawfish, add them as is. Place the pot over hot water and allow the flavors to ripen again, if desired, no more than 10 minutes. Serve the bisque in small cups with buttered toast.

One of the glories of summer—and there are many—is fresh corn, boiled on the cob, cooked in a soup, stewed, or baked with fresh tomatoes, combined with lima beans in succotash, baked in corn pudding, or grilled over coals. One word of warning: Don't add salt to grilled, boiled, or stewed corn until it is tender. Salt toughens fresh corn. And don't overcook corn dishes. They will toughen if you do.

FRESH CORN CHOWDER

[SERVES 4 TO 6]

To catch the full flavor of sweet summertime corn, the chowder should be made very simply.

3	thick slices smoked bacon
1	small onion, chopped
5	potatoes, peeled and chopped
5	cups milk
3	cups tender white corn kernels (6 to 8 ears)
1	tablespoon butter, or to taste
	Salt and freshly ground white pepper to taste
	Chopped fresh parsley, for garnish

1. Sauté the bacon in a skillet over medium heat until done but not overly crisp. Put the bacon aside and add the onion to the skillet. Sauté until the onion is tender and has absorbed the fat, but do not let it brown, 6 to 8 minutes.

2. Combine the potatoes with the cooked onion in a large saucepan and barely cover with water. Boil until the potatoes are tender and the water has boiled low, 20 to 30 minutes.

3. Add the milk, corn, and butter. Simmer, uncovered, about 10 minutes. Add salt and white pepper to taste. Serve piping hot, garnished with a sprinkling of parsley.

VARIATION

• One red or green bell pepper, diced, may be added with the potatoes.

SORREL

Sorrel, the tart, lemony perennial that is grown in all French gardens, is a relative of our sour grass that comes up wild in the spring. A tiny bit of it is enlivening to a green salad, but it is more notable in soup or an omelet—and divine as a stuffing for black bass. Plant a small row and it will greet you happily year after year.

ALABAMA SORREL & POTATO SOUP

[SERVES 4-6]

This could not be called a fine collection of soups if sorrel soup were omitted. The sorrel that grows wild in our meadows in the spring is called sour grass. It is easy to grow in your herb garden, and when cut often it will provision you generously all summer. This is a versatile soup, and the variations are just as delicious—well, almost. Sorrel soup is very special. My favorite way to serve it is in hot weather, well chilled. Swing in a hammock in the shade—read a good book until it lulls you to sleep for a long summer nap. You will think you are back in Alabama.

2	quarts water
2	pounds Idaho potatoes, peeled and cubed (6 cups)
6	tablespoons ($^3/_4$ stick) butter
4	leeks, white part only, rinsed well and thinly sliced ($2^1/_2$ cups)
$^1/_2$	cup cold water
3	cups chopped sorrel leaves
1 – $1^1/_2$	cups milk
	Salt and freshly ground white pepper to taste
	Fresh lemon juice to taste
	Chopped fresh chervil or parsley, for garnish

1. Bring the water to a boil in a large saucepan and add the potato cubes. Simmer, uncovered, until they are tender, about 25 minutes.
2. In the meantime, melt the butter in a heavy stainless-steel or enamel saucepan or soup pot and add the leeks along with the cold water. Allow the leeks to cook until they are limp and the water has boiled away, 5 minutes. (Do not allow the butter to sizzle or the leeks to get the least bit brown.) Stir in the sorrel leaves and cook until they wilt, 1 minute. (They will turn an odd shade of green, but don't worry.)
3. Add the leeks and sorrel to the cooked potatoes and their liquid. Add the milk as needed, starting with 1 cup. Purée in a blender (not a processor) or mash and strain through a sieve. If the soup is too thin, simmer it longer to reduce; if too thick, add more milk. Season with salt and white pepper. Add lemon juice to taste.
4. Pour, piping hot, into a warmed tureen or soup plates. Garnish with a sprinkling of chervil or parsley.

ROASTING AND PEELING PEPPERS

1. Preheat the broiler. 2. Choose perfect peppers that have no dark or soft spots. Wash thoroughly and dry with paper towels. 3. Place the whole peppers in a baking or broiler pan about 4 inches from the heat. Turn the peppers often until they have charred black all over, about 5 minutes. 4. Wrap the peppers in dampened paper towels to steam or place them in a closed paper bag to cool for about 10 minutes. This helps to loosen the skin. 5. When the peppers have cooled, cut them in half. Discard the seeds, membranes, and stems. Peel off the loosened skin with a sharp-pointed paring knife.

Bell peppers can also be charred by holding them on a long cooking fork over a gas flame and turning them frequently until the skins turn black. Follow the directions for steaming and peeling in the above recipe.

SOUP OF THE THREE PEPPERS
[SERVES 4]

This is a very old Southern soup that deserves to be better known. It is very delicate and as beautiful as it is delicious. With a blender or food processor, it is a breeze to make. Serve with dainty cucumber sandwiches, or with a cucumber and dill salad and hot toasted crackers.

2   cups fat-free Rich Chicken Stock (see page 22)
1   jar (4 ounces) whole pimientos, drained
3/4   cup heavy or whipping cream, or more to taste
      Salt to taste
      Tabasco sauce to taste
      Hungarian paprika, for garnish

1. Put 1 cup of the chicken stock in a blender or food processor. Add the pimientos and blend until perfectly smooth. Combine with the remaining cup of chicken stock in a saucepan, and add the cream. Heat just to a boil, season with salt and Tabasco to taste, and sprinkle each serving with a dusting of paprika.

VARIATIONS

*   Add 8 to 10 freshly cooked small shrimp along with the cream, or purée a few with the pimientos and add the rest whole. You may need to add more stock or cream.

DRESSED AND READY

There are two main categories of salad, the composed salad and the green salad. The composed salad's proper place is usually as the main course of a light and informal meal. These salads are enticing to the eye and refreshing to the palate but they are rather substantial, and little else is needed to round out the menu but a good bread, a glass of wine, perhaps, and a delicious dessert. Our top favorites in the South, I believe, are made from chicken, shrimp, or crabmeat tossed in homemade mayonnaise, with celery hearts—more often than not—for crunch and texture.

The joy of any green salad is its talent to refresh, to lend texture and beauty to your menu as well as to lighten it. A mixture of different lettuces, for a variety of texture and taste, dressed with a vinaigrette is superb. But I confess that I have a prejudiced palate: I often serve Bibb lettuce alone as a simple salad with an important meat or as a separate course. Bibb is a world traveler now, but it was born in Kentucky and named for Judge Jack Bibb, who propagated it around 1865 in his hobby greenhouse in Frankfort. It was called limestone lettuce at first, as the alkaline limestone soil of central Kentucky was credited with helping to produce a superior lettuce. The heads of true Bibb lettuce are compact and exquisitely small—one head is a perfect single serving. How did Judge Bibb compose and control the size? What strains of lettuce did he cross to achieve these dainty heads of perfect balance in flavor and texture? No one knows. No one has been able to break the code.

LETTUCE

Leaf lettuce is an early spring favorite that comes along in country gardens with the radishes and scallions. This famous trilogy tossed in a bowl with crisp smoked bacon and a touch of vinegar is dear to the heart of every Southerner. The ruffled, sweet leaves are highly perishable and should be used the day the lettuce is gathered or purchased. It is a poor choice for a garnish. Red leaf lettuce is a member of the same family.

Boston, a soft, flavorful lettuce, is one of the best of all the lettuces if it is to be used alone for a salad. It also combines well, however, with crisp romaine and endive. Only the beautiful yellow inside leaves (or heart) are useful in garnishing.

SHADY LANE SALAD

[SERVES 4]

In the heart of the bluegrass country there is an old curved road, seldom traveled now, that goes from Frankfort to Lexington. There are vine-covered stone fences on either side of this road, built long ago by slave labor and still strong and beautiful. Large trees bend over the road, forming a canopy of protection from the sun. We take this narrow old road very slowly so we can drink in the beauty of the rolling land and farm pastures where the Thoroughbred horses romp. Many times, if we stop, the high-spirited mares come up to peep over the fence to see what's going on. When they decide that all is well, they toss their gorgeous heads and fly away. What elegance.

I never intended to let a spring blend into summer without a day's outing to drive along Shady Lane to Lexington. I haven't missed many.

4   heads Bibb lettuce, or 1 to 2 heads Boston or other leaf lettuce
1   center slice country ham
4   hard-cooked eggs, sliced
1^1/$_2$ tablespoons capers, drained
^{1}/$_3$ cup chopped chives or tender scallion (green onion) tops
      Chopped fresh marjoram, chervil, and tarragon, for garnish

VINAIGRETTE
^{1}/$_3$ cup good-quality olive or vegetable oil
1^1/$_2$ tablespoons white or red wine vinegar

1.   Separate the lettuce, rinse it, and dry in a spinner.
2.   Cut the ham into slivers. Grease an iron skillet well with a piece of ham or bacon fat. Sauté the ham quickly.
3.   In the meantime, put the lettuce in a salad bowl. Scatter the eggs and capers about. Put the ham slivers in the center. Add the chives or scallion tops and the fresh herbs.
4.   Blend the vinaigrette ingredients together with a whisk.
5.   Present the salad, then add the dressing, toss, and serve.

•   Delicious with bread, corn muffins, biscuits, or hot rolls for luncheon, or with tender ears of corn dripping with butter for a light supper on the patio.

BROCCOLI

Broccoli has an assertive flavor. It never fades into the background. It has grown in favor with Americans because it is companionable with steak, roast beef, chicken, ham, and fish—and it is easy to prepare.

In selecting broccoli at the market, look for the bunches that have slender stems and tight, dark green flower buds. If the flower buds are the least bit yellow, the broccoli is past its prime. Don't buy it.

WARM BROCCOLI & RED BELL PEPPER SALAD

[SERVES 4 TO 6]

Serve this gorgeous Southern salad with veal chops or roast, broiled chicken, or steak.

1	bunch broccoli
2	red bell peppers, cored and seeded
1	sweet yellow banana pepper, cored and seeded
$1/2$	cup homemade mayonnaise (see page 60)
$1/2$	cup sour cream
2	ounces Roquefort or Danish blue cheese, at room temperature
	Salt to taste
$1/2$	cup black olives (Niçoise type is best here), or $1^1/2$ tablespoons capers, well drained
4	hard-cooked eggs, quartered
	Chopped fresh parsley, chervil, or tarragon, for garnish
$1/3$	cup Classic Vinaigrette (see page 61)

1. Peel the stems of the broccoli. Divide the head into serving pieces. Set aside.
2. Cut the red and yellow peppers into thin slivers. Set aside.
3. Blend the mayonnaise, sour cream, and Roquefort in a small bowl. Add salt if needed.
4. Drop the broccoli into boiling salted water to cover. Cook until tender but still crisp and green, 8 to 10 minutes, depending on the freshness of the broccoli. Drain well. Transfer to a warmed shallow platter making a pleasing design. Sprinkle the pepper slivers over the broccoli. Place the black olives in a mound in the center of the platter, if you are using them. Arrange the eggs around the platter and sprinkle them with chopped parsley, chervil, or tarragon, salt, and capers, if you are using them.
5. Spoon the vinaigrette over the warm broccoli. Serve with a sauceboat of the mayonnaise mixture.

VARIATION

• If you like anchovies, 3 or 4 may be chopped and added to the vinaigrette dressing, or they can be passed separately in a small bowl.

ZUCCHINI & PARSLEY SALAD
[SERVES 6]

Parsley salads are fabulous for summer patio and barbecue parties with grilled meats of all kinds, and they are also delicious for a family dinner in the kitchen with hamburgers.

	5 or 6 very small firm zucchini
	6 to 8 cherry tomatoes
1	cup chopped Italian (flat-leaf) parsley
1	cup chopped curly parsley
	Classic Vinaigrette to taste (see page 61)
	Salt to taste
$1/4$	cup chopped fresh basil leaves, or more to taste

1. Slice the zucchini into julienne strips not larger than matchsticks. You should have $1^1/2$ cups. Cut the tomatoes in half. Toss the zucchini and tomatoes gently with all the parsley. Season with the dressing and sprinkle with salt. (No pepper should be added when using basil.) Toss gently. Sprinkle with fresh basil leaves.

VIDALIA ONION SALAD
[SERVES 6]

Thinly sliced onions are delicious with hamburgers or grilled steak or chops.

1	large red onion
1	large Spanish onion
$1/2$	cup vegetable oil
2	tablespoons white wine vinegar, or more to taste
1	teaspoon fresh lemon juice
	Salt and freshly ground black pepper to taste
2	tablespoons chopped fresh parsley
2	tablespoons chopped fresh chives

1. Peel the onions and cut into thin slices. Lay the slices in a dish in an attractive design.
2. Mix together the oil, vinegar, lemon juice, and salt and pepper. Taste and correct the seasoning as needed. Pour the dressing over the onions and sprinkle them with parsley and chives.

FRESH LIMA & GREEN BEAN SALAD

[SERVES 4]

For really tender green beans, select the ones that are pencil thin and brittle. Check to see if they "snap" when they are bent; if they don't, they are not fresh. Instead of stringing beans or cutting them through the middle, slice off the side seams and the ends very judiciously. This leaves the tender portion intact. So-called "frenching" makes green beans watery. If beans have developed inside the pod, it has grown beyond the salad or quick-cooking stage and should be prepared in other ways.

2	cups fresh lima beans
$^1/_4$	pound small tender green or yellow wax beans
5	slices lean smoked bacon
$^1/_4$	cup chopped red bell pepper
2	tablespoons chopped fresh tarragon
2	tablespoons chopped fresh parsley
$^3/_4$	cup Tangy Mustard Vinaigrette (see page 61)

1. Preheat the oven to 425°F.
2. Cook the lima beans in boiling salted water to cover until tender but not mushy, 20 to 25 minutes. Drain thoroughly.
3. With a sharp knife, trim stringy edges and ends off the green or wax beans. (This ensures their tenderness.) Cook in boiling salted water to cover until tender but still somewhat crisp, 7 to 10 minutes. Drain the beans thoroughly.
4. In the meantime, cook the bacon on a baking sheet in the oven for 10 to 12 minutes. Do not allow it to get overly crisp. Drain on paper towels, then chop.
5. Blanch the red bell pepper in $^1/_2$ cup boiling water for 1 to 2 minutes. Drain.
6. Combine the beans, bell pepper, tarragon, and parsley.
7. Toss the salad with the dressing and the bacon just before serving so the tarragon and parsley will remain fresh and green and the bacon will not become limp.

- The salad may be presented on a large platter surrounded by sliced tomatoes, and accompanied by corn muffins or your favorite homemade bread.

MORE HERBS THAT ARE DELICIOUS IN SALADS

FRENCH TARRAGON: Few herbs lend their flavor and fragrance to summer salads more readily than tarragon. And what would we do without tarragon vinegar all year long?

THYME: Fresh thyme does not blend with every salad, as it is often too intense, but a touch of thyme is special in meat salads.

POTATO SALADS

I like to use new, or waxy, potatoes when the recipe calls for a mayonnaise dressing.

When the dressing is a vinaigrette or a warm dressing, mealy potatoes, such as Idaho potatoes, are best because they absorb the dressing better.

AVOCADO, APPLE & GRAPEFRUIT SALAD
[SERVES 6]

A delicious winter salad when these fruits are the best available. Notable with lamb. If you wish, try it sometime with The Breakers Sunshine Dressing below.

2	avocados, peeled and sliced
1	apple (Red or Golden Delicious), peeled and sliced
2	navel oranges, peeled and cut into sections
1	grapefruit, peeled and cut into sections
12 – 18	leaves Bibb or Boston lettuce or endive
6	tablespoons olive or vegetable oil
1	teaspoon Dijon mustard
2	tablespoons fresh grapefruit juice
1	tablespoon white wine vinegar, or to taste
	Salt to taste

Put the avocado and apple slices and the orange and grapefruit sections on a bed of lettuce.
Mix the remaining ingredients in a small bowl and pour over the fruit when ready to serve.

THE BREAKERS SUNSHINE DRESSING
[MAKES ABOUT 1 CUP]

$1/2$	cup fresh lemon juice
$1/2$	cup good-quality vegetable oil
2	tablespoons sugar
$1/4$	teaspoon salt

Beat all ingredients thoroughly with a whisk and serve on fruit salads.

CHICORY

Curly chicory is a kind of endive. The beautiful shades of light green and yellow make chicory a lovely garnishing lettuce. Its bitter tang and curly leaves are invaluable in a mixed green salad and are especially attractive when combined with Belgian endive. It is of little value when not properly pale, as the dark green leaves are bitter.

NEW POTATO SALAD
WITH ASPARAGUS & CHICORY

[SERVES 6]

The divine combination of new potatoes and fresh asparagus is a gastronome's delight. To give it the place of honor it deserves, use it as an entrée for a light Sunday night supper or a luncheon. It is also delicious with a slice of baked country ham, broiled chicken, or a rare steak.

$2^1/_2$ pounds new potatoes, peeled, boiled, and cooled
$^3/_4$ cup homemade mayonnaise (see page 60) made with tarragon vinegar
12   spears fresh green asparagus, cooked
2   tablespoons Classic Vinaigrette (see page 61) made with lemon juice
     Pale chicory or Bibb lettuce, for garnish
6   hard-cooked eggs, quartered, for garnish
2   tablespoons chopped fresh tarragon
     Salt and freshly ground white pepper to taste

1.   Slice the potatoes and toss them with the mayonnaise.
2.   In a separate bowl, season the asparagus with the Classic Vinaigrette.
3.   Mound the potatoes in the center of a round platter. Surround with asparagus spears. Garnish the platter with lettuce and the hard-cooked eggs. Sprinkle the entire salad with fresh tarragon and salt and white pepper to taste.

THE GOOD BERRY

Connoisseurs place our native wild rice among the great foods of the world. It is not a rice at all but a grain that grows wild around the lakes of Wisconsin and Minnesota. It is still harvested there as Indians did of old, by men gliding along in canoes. They bend the tall stalks and thrash them in such a way that the ripe grains fall into the boat. This is an expensive process, but wild rice is divine food even if it is luxurious. The Indians called it manomin, "the good berry." Indeed it is.

WILD RICE SALAD

[SERVES 6]

1^{1}/$_{2}$ cups wild rice, uncooked
^{1}/$_{2}$ pound fresh crisp mushrooms, cleaned and slivered
3   tablespoons chopped fresh marjoram
^{1}/$_{2}$ cup chopped fresh parsley (Italian, if possible)
2   tablespoons chopped chives or tender scallion (green onion) tops
^{2}/$_{3}$ cup Tangy Mustard Vinaigrette (see page 61) made with red wine vinegar, or more to taste
    Salt and freshly ground black pepper to taste
    Sprigs of marjoram, parsley, or watercress, for garnish

1. Wash the wild rice thoroughly, rinsing it 6 to 8 times. Drop it into boiling salted water and boil until al dente, or firm to the bite, 30 to 40 minutes. Drain at once. Cool.

2. A short while before serving, toss the rice with the mushrooms, marjoram, parsley, chives or scallion tops, and enough vinaigrette to moisten it well. Taste. Add salt and pepper if needed.

3. Place in a salad bowl and garnish with sprigs of watercress, parsley, or, best of all, marjoram.

VARIATION

- Combine 1^{1}/$_{4}$ cups wild rice, 5 or 6 chopped anchovy fillets, ^{1}/$_{2}$ pound slivered crisp fresh mushrooms, 1 clove garlic mashed and marinated in ^{2}/$_{3}$ cup vinaigrette (sieve out the garlic before using the dressing), 3 tablespoons chopped fresh marjoram leaves, and ^{1}/$_{2}$ cup pitted Niçoise or Greek black olives. My favorite. Delicious with veal roast, scaloppini, steak, or rare rib or sirloin roast.

RICH VINAIGRETTE

[MAKES 1 CUP]

This is a popular variation on the Classic Vinaigrette, and it can be made in a blender. The herbs should complement the menu—use tarragon with veal, chicken, or fish, and sweet basil with beef. Parsley and chervil are pleasant with all dishes.

1   egg yolk

2   tablespoons white wine vinegar

1   tablespoon Dijon mustard

³/₄ cup good-quality olive or
    vegetable oil

    Salt and freshly ground white
    pepper to taste

    Fresh lemon juice, if needed

    Bouquet of mixed chopped fresh
    herbs, 2 tablespoons each
    (see headnote)

Combine the egg yolk, vinegar, mustard, oil, salt, and white pepper in a blender. Mix well. Taste, and add more salt and a squeeze of lemon juice if needed. Add herbs to taste.

COUNTRY GARDEN SLAW

[SERVES 6]

You can choreograph this salad to your taste. Green cabbage, cauliflower, and an assortment of herbs may also be used.

5   carrots, peeled

6   small firm zucchini

1   cucumber, sliced thin and slivered

4   celery hearts, sliced thin

1   green bell pepper, cored, seeded, and chopped

1   red bell pepper or 1 sweet yellow banana pepper, cored, seeded, and slivered
    Salt to taste

¹/₂ cup chopped fresh parsley

¹/₄ cup chopped fresh basil, or more to taste

³/₄ cup (approximately) Classic or Rich Vinaigrette (see page 61 and sidebar, respectively)

Cut the carrots and zucchini into matchsticks. Mix with the cucumber, celery, and peppers, and add salt to taste. Add the parsley and basil. Toss with the dressing and serve.

•   When fresh basil is out of season, use a basil wine vinegar or add a generous amount of French Dijon mustard. French basil is sufficiently peppery without adding black pepper. When fresh herbs are out of season, use a large handful of chopped parsley. Green is in.

CRAB NORFOLK SALAD

[SERVES 4]

In Virginia and Maryland, Crab Norfolk has long been a great favorite—one of our best dishes, and thoroughly indigenous to native American cuisine. Crabmeat Norfolk teams so well with rice that I make an entrée salad with the combination, or you can create a chic and delectable salad using orzo (small pasta shaped like rice). Both are pleasing served cold or warm, and they are excellent as a first course. A true Crab Norfolk is never seasoned with garlic or onions, nor is the sauce thickened with flour or egg yolks, which rob it of its lightness.

1	pound fresh blackfin lump crabmeat
1	cup long-grain rice
5	tablespoons unsalted butter
3	thin slices baked country ham, slivered
1/2	cup heavy or whipping cream, or as needed
2	tablespoons chopped fresh tarragon
	Salt if needed
	Cayenne pepper to taste
2	bunches watercress, 3 heads Bibb lettuce, or 1 large head Boston lettuce
	Chopped fresh tarragon, chervil, and parsley, for garnish
1	lemon, cut into wedges

1. Pick over the crabmeat well, discarding any cartilage. Leave the pieces as large as possible.
2. Cook the rice until tender but still al dente, or firm to the bite. Keep warm.
3. Melt 3 tablespoons of the butter in a heavy enamel or stainless-steel skillet. Add the crabmeat and toss it lightly in the butter. Add the ham and mix well. Add just enough cream to make a small amount of sauce. (It should bind the crabmeat and ham lightly. When served, the sauce should not drown the rice or run over the plate.)
4. When ready to serve, toss the warm rice with the remaining butter and the tarragon. Add salt, if desired (the ham is salty), and cayenne pepper.
5. Line 4 salad plates with watercress or lettuce. Spoon the warm tarragon rice onto the lettuce. Make a small well in the center of the rice and fill it with the crabmeat and ham mixture. Sprinkle chopped fresh herbs over the entire dish. Garnish each plate with a wedge of lemon (to squeeze over the lettuce as well as the crabmeat).

VARIATION

- Omit the ham and season the rice with imported Madras curry powder. Sprinkle with a few buttered toasted slivered almonds or toasted pine nuts. Sprinkle chopped fresh coriander over the crabmeat just before serving.

TO COOK RICE IN ADVANCE

Steam or boil the rice, drain it well if it was boiled, and fluff it with a fork. Taste for salt. Allow the rice to get cold, then put it in a shallow overproof dish. Cover with foil and refrigerate. (The rice must be cold before it is covered with foil or it will steam and become soggy.)

When you are ready to serve the rice, transfer it, leaving the foil intact, to a preheated 325°F oven and bake for about 30 minutes. Remove the foil, fluff the rice with a fork, add butter and seasonings, and serve.

THE DRESSINGS
FOR SALADS

The dressings for salads are very simple, really. Most salads require a vinaigrette dressing, which combines an excellent oil (the most flavorful is Italian or French olive oil, or an imported nut oil, such as walnut or hazelnut) with an acid, which complements the ingredients of the salad and adds a zest and spark to the oil. The nature and flavor of these oils and acids vary and should blend with the chosen salad. A salad of delicate lettuce leaves should have a mild dressing, for instance; a hearty salad with beef or ham calls for an assertive mustardy dressing. All of these things you learn through trial and triumph, or through trial and error, remembering the next time what you did to make the previous salad so great, or what you think led the salad astray.

The traditional dressings for salads other than vinaigrette are cream dressings and mayonnaise. With a little practice, you will get the hang of all three and will then always make your own. Bottled vinaigrette is more expensive than homemade and is anathema to a good cook. Your own will be so much better.

MAYONNAISE

[MAKES 2¼ CUPS]

This is the classic way to make mayonnaise. A whisk can be used instead of a mixer. Wine vinegar can be substituted for lemon juice, but the dressing will not be as delicate. Note: no sugar.

2   egg yolks, at room temperature
½   teaspoon salt, or to taste
1   tablespoon fresh lemon juice, or more to taste
½   teaspoon dry mustard
2   cups good-quality vegetable oil, at room temperature
2   tablespoons boiling water
    Dash of cayenne pepper

1. Put the egg yolks, salt, lemon juice, and mustard in the small bowl of an electric mixer, or use a bowl for a hand mixer. Beat until slightly thickened, about 5 minutes.

2. Start adding the oil, 1 teaspoon at a time, beating continuously. Watch closely and do not add more oil until the last addition has been absorbed.

3. After 1 cup of oil has been added and you have a thick emulsion, the oil may be added a bit faster, such as a tablespoon or two at a time, until all of it has been incorporated. Add the boiling water, still beating continuously.

4. Taste the mayonnaise for lemon juice and salt. Add more if desired, and a dash of cayenne.

• If the oil is added to the yolks too fast at any time, the emulsion will be broken and the mayonnaise will curdle. Keep a small pan of boiling water on the stove during the whole process of making mayonnaise. Watch the mayonnaise closely. If it starts to separate or curdle, add a tablespoon or so of boiling water, beating fast.

If the emulsion separates completely, you will have to start over: Put the curdled mixture in a glass measuring pitcher or bowl. Add enough oil to make 2 cups; mix well. Put 1 egg yolk (room temperature) in a clean, dry bowl. Add a tiny bit of salt and lemon juice. Beat until the yolk thickens a bit. Then start adding the curdled mixture, 1 teaspoon at a time, beating continuously. Slowly—slowly. Gradually an emulsion will be formed. Add all of the curdled mixture, then complete by adding 2 tablespoons boiling water. This will be a richer mayonnaise with the extra yolk, but it will be good. As you become more experienced, you can add ½ cup extra oil to cut the richness of the extra yolk.

BLENDER MAYO

[MAKES 1½ CUPS]

The electric blender is still one of our best kitchen gadgets. In many cases it is better than a food processor, as in making a small amount of mayonnaise. The method given here makes a delightful mayonnaise, and it is the quickest of all.

1   whole egg, at room temperature

1   egg yolk, at room temperature

1   cup good-quality flavorless vegetable oil (or use part olive oil if you wish), at room temperature

½   teaspoon (scant) salt

½   teaspoon dry mustard (Colman's is excellent)

2   tablespoons fresh lemon juice, or to taste
    Cayenne pepper to taste

1. Put the whole egg, egg yolk, ¼ cup of the oil, the salt, mustard, and lemon juice in a blender. Turn the motor on. After a minute, start pouring in more of the remaining oil in a thin stream.

2. After using about half of the oil, stop the blender, remove the cover, and stir the mayonnaise with a long-handled spoon. Turn the blender on again and continue to add the oil slowly. If at any time a puddle of oil accumulates at the top of the mayonnaise, shut off the blender and stir the mayonnaise well with the long-handled spoon.

3. Taste the mayonnaise for salt and lemon juice, and correct if necessary. Add cayenne pepper to taste.

•   The purpose of making mayonnaise in small amounts is to always use freshly made mayonnaise, which is far superior.

•   If the mayonnaise is too thick for your taste, add a tablespoon of boiling water just before finishing it up.

•   A small amount of white wine vinegar may be used with or instead of the lemon juice. Generally, lemon juice is the best acid for mayonnaise, but tarragon vinegar can be delicious in mayonnaise for chicken or seafood salad.

CLASSIC VINAIGRETTE

[MAKES 1 CUP]

In making all vinaigrettes, the vinegar or lemon juice, salt, pepper, and any other seasoning must be combined before the oil is added. All vinaigrettes are at their best when made just before serving.

¼   cup good-quality vinegar or fresh lemon juice

    Salt and freshly ground black pepper to taste

¾   cup good-quality olive or vegetable oil, or more to taste

1. Combine the vinegar or lemon juice, salt, and pepper in a small bowl.

2. Gradually whisk in the oil to taste.

•   Many types of vinegar can be used: white wine, red wine, or any of the herb-flavored wines, such as tarragon.

VINAIGRETTE PLUS

[MAKES 2¼ CUPS]

Garlic Vinaigrette: Allow 1 clove garlic to marinate in 1 cup Classic Vinaigrette from 12 to 24 hours. Remove the garlic.

Warm Vinaigrette: To 1 cup Classic Vinaigrette, add 2 chopped hard-cooked eggs, 1 tablespoon each chopped fresh parsley and chives, and 1 teaspoon dry mustard. Serve hot over broccoli, fresh green asparagus, or hot potato salad.

TANGY MUSTARD VINAIGRETTE

[MAKES 1 CUP]

For artichokes, asparagus, and all salads that need the flavorful blessings of a good mustard.

⅓   cup white vinegar

⅔   cup good-quality olive oil, or ⅓ cup olive oil and ⅓ cup vegetable oil.

1½ teaspoons light yellow Dijon mustard, or more to taste

⅔   teaspoon salt, or more to taste

•   Combine the ingredients in a blender and and mix well. If using a whisk, combine all the ingredients except the oil in a small bowl. Gradually add the oil, whisking briskly.

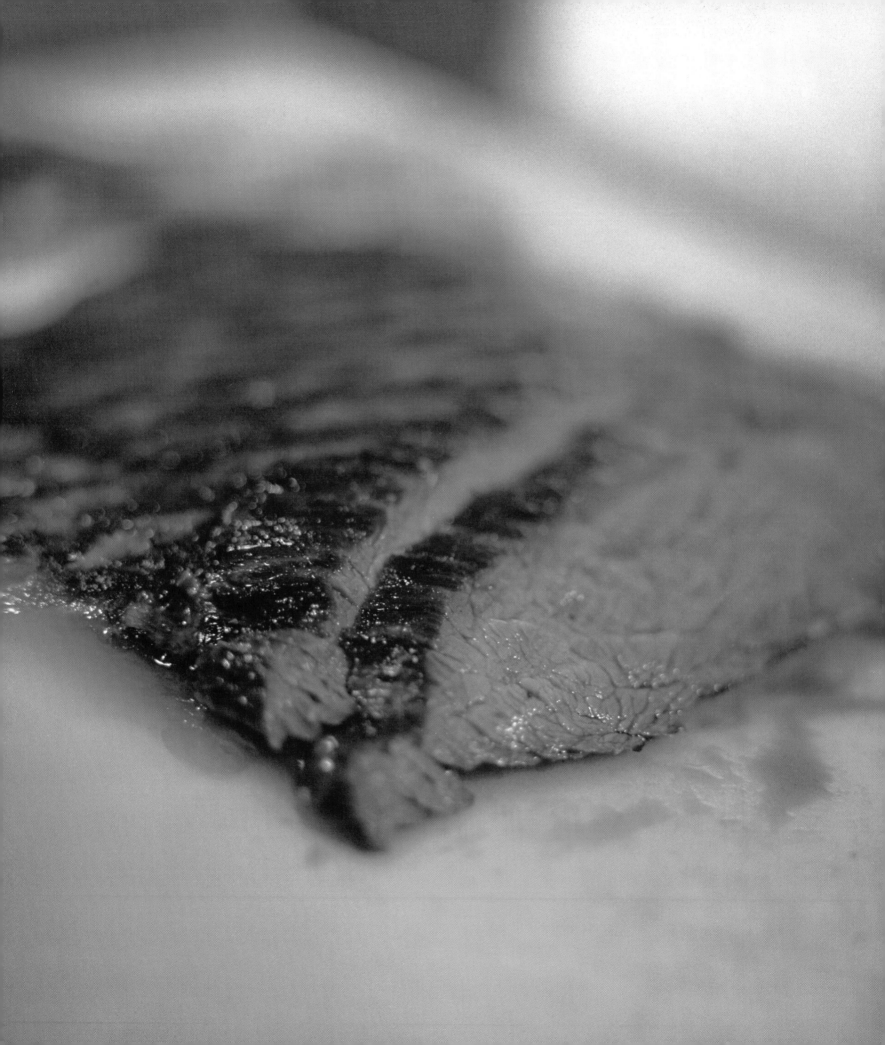

ALL MANNER OF MEN LOVE MEAT

In my long years of cooking, I have never doubted for a minute that fine food enhances the quality of life. And one of the favorite foods of the great family of man is the pleasing taste of good meat. Although meat is very expensive now, you do not have to have it every day. But when you do have it, cook it with care.

Successful meat cookery begins in the market, and the key to it is recognizing good-quality meat when you see it, or finding a knowledgeable butcher who will help you. If you find one, you are fortunate; remain loyal to his shop.

In choosing which meat to buy, the most important decision of all is the menu. The vegetable, salad, bread, and dessert must be compatible with that meat. They must taste good together. It is as simple as that.

HOW TO COOK A COUNTRY HAM

[SERVES 25 TO 30]

A cooked country smoked ham keeps under refrigeration much better than most any meat, but it does not freeze well. There are dozens of recipes, but a really good country ham only needs to be cooked in water. No fancy recipe will make a good ham out of a bad one. Note that you'll need to begin preparing the ham two days before you get a bite of it.

1 whole smoked country ham, about 15 pounds
2 tablespoons ground cloves
$^2/_3$ cup light brown sugar
   Medium-dry to dry sherry or red wine or cider vinegar (see step 8)

1. Scrub the ham thoroughly with a stiff brush.
2. Place the ham in a large pot or pan or even in a picnic cooler and cover it completely with water. Allow it to soak for 12 to 24 hours. Discard the water.
3. Preheat the oven to 325°F.
4. Put the ham in a large roaster, fat side up, and again cover completely with water. Place in the oven on the lowest shelf and bake for 2 hours. Do not allow the water to exceed a gentle simmer at any time. If necessary, lower the oven heat.
5. At the end of the 2 hours, turn the ham on its other side and cook another 2 hours, so it will cook evenly throughout. It takes 4 to 4$^1/_2$ hours in all, or 15 to 18 minutes per pound for a tender ham. An instant-reading thermometer inserted in the meaty part should read 170°F when the ham is done.
6. Remove the ham from the oven, but leave it in the water overnight (not refrigerated). (This procedure is important to help ensure a moist ham.)
7. The next day, preheat the oven to 425°F.
8. Remove and discard the ham skin. Sprinkle the fat with the ground cloves. Combine the light brown sugar with just enough sherry or vinegar to make a paste, and brush this mixture over the top of the ham.
9. Bake the ham until it has a beautiful golden glaze, 20 to 30 minutes. Allow the ham to rest for 1 hour or more, then slice it very, very thin.

KEEPING HAM

After baking, a properly smoked country ham will keep well refrigerated for 4 to 5 weeks. After that time, place the ham, or what is left of it, back in a 325°F oven and heat thoroughly for 1 to 1$^1/_2$ hours. The ham will then keep for another 4 to 5 weeks under refrigeration.

STUFFED POACHED APPLES

6   large apples (Golden Delicious,
    Granny Smith, or Rome Beauty)

1½ cups water

2   thin slices lemon

1   small slice fresh ginger or
    small piece dried ginger (optional)

¾   cup sugar, approximately

1   cup boiling water

6   dried prunes or apricots

1. Peel and core the apples. Trim a thin slice off the bottoms so they will sit steady. 2. Combine water, lemon slices, ginger, and sugar in a fairly deep heavy pan and bring to a simmer. Place the apples in the seasoned water and simmer, basting almost constantly, until they become transparent, about 30 minutes in all. Do not let the syrup boil or the apples will not hold their shape. Transfer the apples to a shallow dish and allow them to cool. Reserve the syrup. 3. Pour the boiling water over the dried fruit and let it soak until plump, 15 minutes. 4. Gently stuff the center of each apple with a prune or apricot. Before serving, reheat the apples in a preheated 300°F oven. Heat the syrup and spoon some over the apples to make them shine.

STUFFED PORK CHOPS

[SERVES 6]

Every cut of fresh pork, even chops, prospers by slow, even, moist cooking—exuding its own flavors and mingling with herbs in a pleasing broth.

    Flavorful Pork Stuffing (recipe follows)
6   double-thick pork loin chops
    Salt to taste
¼   cup all-purpose flour
4   tablespoons (½ stick) butter
    Freshly ground black pepper to taste
⅔   cup Chicken Stock (see page 38)
    Stuffed Poached Apples (see sidebar)
    Chopped fresh parsley, for garnish

1. Preheat the oven to 325°F.

2. Prepare the stuffing.

3. Make a pocket in each pork chop with a sharp knife.

4. Fill the pockets of the pork chops with the stuffing. Close each chop with toothpicks. Season with salt and dust with flour on both sides.

5. Melt the butter in a heavy ovenproof skillet over medium-high heat. Add the chops and sauté until both sides are golden brown. Do not cook them any further. Season with pepper, add the chicken stock, and cover the skillet with a lid or foil.

6. Place the skillet in the oven and bake until the chops are extremely tender, 30 to 40 minutes.

7. Serve with Stuffed Poached Apples and garnish with parsley.

FLAVORFUL PORK STUFFING:

•   In a large skillet brown the breadcrumbs lightly in 1 tablespoon of the melted butter. Add the remaining melted butter, celery, parsley, and rosemary or marjoram. Moisten with just enough chicken stock to hold the crumbs together. Season with salt and pepper.

COOKING PORK AND HAM

A great deal of our native Southern cuisine has been built on the glories of the pig. We enjoy pork in every fashion—from crown roasts to spareribs and sausages spiced with plenty of pepper, sage, or rosemary. But when I'm asked to name the South's most illustrious meat dish, our country hams quickly come to mind. They are reputed to be unique in the world of smoked meat, with a very special flavor. The men who process the finest of them are as proud of their craft and art as the vintage winemakers, and they guard their methods well.

BARBECUED SPARERIBS

[SERVES 6]

Barbecued spareribs should be braised first in the oven. They will grill more quickly, will be tender and juicy, and the sauce will not burn.

2	sides small, tender, meaty pork spareribs, 3 pounds each
2	cups cold water
1	small onion, sliced
1	bay leaf
$^1/_2$	teaspoon dried thyme or several sprigs fresh
2	tablespoons butter, at room temperature, or $^1/_4$ cup vegetable oil
	Salt and freshly ground black pepper to taste
	Barbecue sauce (see step 5)

1. Preheat the oven to 350°F.
2. Place the ribs in a roasting pan with the water, onion, bay leaf, and thyme. Cover and cook in the oven until the meat is tender, 35 to 40 minutes.
3. Meanwhile, prepare the grill by placing an oiled rack 4 to 6 inches over hot mesquite or hickory chips.
4. Remove the ribs from the pan juices. Brush thoroughly with the butter and season with salt and pepper. Grill briskly until crisp but still juicy, 6 to 7 minutes total. Serve with a barbecue sauce on the side.
5. Or brush the ribs with vegetable oil and place them over a brisk fire. As soon as they begin to brown, baste them with Talmadge Farm Barbecue Sauce or Kentucky Heirloom Barbecue Sauce (see page 84). Baste them quickly on both sides and do not allow the sauce to char, 3 to 4 minutes total.

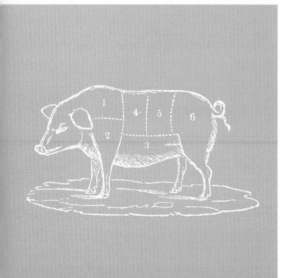

BARBECUED BONED LEG OF LAMB

[SERVES 8 TO 10 GENEROUSLY]

To many gourmets, the tender meat of young lamb has no peer in outdoor cooking. The choice cuts of lamb come from the hindquarters—the legs and both the large and small loins.

Actually, any cut of meat that can be roasted successfully (roasting is cooking with dry heat) can be barbecued, and lamb lends itself most graciously to many sauces and combinations of food.

$^1/_4$	cup dry red wine
2	tablespoons good-quality olive or salad oil
1	tablespoon crushed dried rosemary or marjoram
$^1/_2$	onion, sliced
	Juice of 1 lemon
1	leg of lamb, 6 to 7 pounds, boned
3	slices smoked bacon
	Salt and freshly ground black pepper to taste
	Kentucky Heirloom Barbecue Sauce (see page 84)

VEGETABLES THAT ARE GOOD WITH LAMB

Artichokes

Asparagus

Carrots

Dried White Beans

Eggplant

Green Beans

Lima Beans

Mushrooms

Onions

Peas

Tomatoes

White potatoes

Zucchini

1. In a small bowl, combine the wine, oil, rosemary or marjoram, onion, and lemon juice.
2. Cut 3 deep incisions in the thickest part of the meat. Dip each piece of bacon into the marinade and then roll it up and insert it deep into one of the incisions.
3. Place the lamb in a large bowl or heavy polyethylene bag, pour the marinade over it, and cover the bowl or tie the bag. Marinate the meat in the refrigerator overnight or for 24 hours.
4. Next day, prepare the grill.
5. Lift the lamb from the marinade and dry it with paper towels. Salt and pepper it well, and fold the meat into a compact shape, tucking in the ends. Skewer the meat together with long metal or wooden skewers, sliding one in lengthwise and one in crosswise.
6. Place the lamb on the grill or on a rotisserie, at least 18 inches above the heat. Allow the meat to cook until almost done, then baste it with the barbecue sauce.

• It is necessary to have the meat 18 inches above the heat when using a basting sauce that contains ketchup or brown sugar, as it will burn otherwise.

OLD SEELBACH HOUSE
TENDERLOIN CHUNKS

[SERVES 4 TO 6]

This is an herb-filled tomato steak sauce for all seasons. Delightful with tenderloin, delicious with hamburgers. Grill the beef in the summer; sauté it in a skillet in the winter. Serve with French-fried potatoes, baked potatoes, scalloped potatoes, or Potatoes Anna—and parsley and red cabbage slaw. Eat... eat... eat! Live... live... live!

BARBECUE

In the South, the word "barbecue" brings to mind the taste of ketchup, Worcestershire sauce, onions, cayenne pepper, and Tabasco, because that is the way the meat has traditionally been seasoned. A barbecue, however, really means any meat, fish, or fowl that is cooked over the coals or on a spit—not necessarily basted with a highly seasoned sauce.

$^1/_3$ pound beef kidney suet

2   pounds beef tenderloin or sirloin, cut into $1^1/_2$- to 2-inch cubes

    Salt and freshly ground black pepper to taste

    Old Seelbach House Steak Sauce (see page 85), heated

    Chopped fresh parsley, for garnish

1. Put the suet in a very hot black iron skillet. Add the meat and sauté it quickly over high heat, about 3 to 4 minutes. Turn the pieces to brown on all sides, but keep them rare. Season with salt and pepper.

2. Put several spoonfuls of piping-hot sauce in the center of each warm dinner plate and lay chunks of steak in the center of the sauce. Sprinkle with parsley. Work fast to serve everything very hot.

OYSTERS & TENDERLOIN EN BROCHETTE

[SERVES 4]

We have dozens of ways to prepare oysters in the South, but there are no skewered dishes more elegant than oysters and tenderloin. For formal parties, serve them accompanied by the Mustard and Tarragon Hollandaise and white wine. For informal parties, serve them with Old Seelbach House Steak Sauce and cold beer.

MUSTARD AND TARRAGON HOLLANDAISE

[MAKES 1^1/2 CUPS]

2   hard-cooked egg yolks, mashed

2   raw egg yolks

2   teaspoons light yellow
    Dijon mustard, or more to taste

3   tablespoons tarragon vinegar

1   teaspoon salt, or to taste

1^1/4 cups good-quality olive oil,
    vegetable oil, or hot, melted,
    unsalted butter
    Cayenne pepper to taste

Put the hard-cooked egg yolks in a blender, food processor, or a roomy bowl. Add the raw egg yolks, mustard, vinegar, and salt. With the machine running, or while beating, gradually blend in the oil or melted butter. Taste for salt. Add cayenne to taste.

16   fresh large oysters (allow 4 per person), shucked (see Index)

8   slices smoked bacon, cut in half

4 – 5 tablespoons unsalted butter, melted
     Salt to taste

1   tablespoon chopped fresh marjoram leaves or 1 teaspoon dried

16   large mushroom caps (allow 1 per oyster)

1   pound beef tenderloin, cut into 1-inch chunks
     Freshly ground black pepper to taste

2   cups chopped fresh parsley, or as needed
     Mustard and Tarragon Hollandaise (see sidebar), Old Seelbach House Steak Sauce (see page 85), or lemon wedges

1.   Preheat the oven to 450°F.

2.   Drain the oysters. (Reserve the liquor, which can be frozen for later use.) Lay the oysters on paper towels or a clean cloth to absorb the excess moisture. Wrap each oyster in a piece of bacon. Secure with a toothpick.

3.   Season the melted butter with salt and marjoram, and dip the mushroom caps into the butter mixture. Thread the buttered mushrooms, on thin short skewers, alternating with the bacon-covered oysters. Thread the tenderloin chunks on identical skewers.

4.   Place the oyster-and-mushroom-filled skewers in a shallow pan in the oven and cook until the bacon has cooked through but is not overly crisp, about 20 to 25 minutes. After the oysters have cooked for 10 to 15 minutes, brush the tenderloin-filled skewers with some of the butter and place them in a separate pan in the oven. (The tenderloin must stay rare, and it cooks faster than the bacon.)

5.   When the tenderloin-filled skewers have cooked for 6 to 8 minutes, turn them so they will cook evenly. When the beef is done but still pink, remove all the skewers from the oven—not over 3 minutes more. Season with salt and freshly ground pepper.

6.   Warm individual plates and place a skewer of tenderloin chunks and a skewer of oysters and mushrooms on a bed of chopped parsley for each serving. Pass a sauceboat of Mustard and Tarragon Hollandaise, Old Seelbach House Steak Sauce, or, if desired, wedges of lemon.

COOKING BEEF

There is a different cut of beef appropriate to every meal of the day and for most occasions, from Southern country stews and pot roasts to tenderloin for elegant dinners.

A premium beef will be well marbled, with tiny veins of fat running through it, and the fat on the outside will be creamy white and very firm. Yellow fat indicates poor quality beef. Rib roasts, tenderloin, and steaks are the luxurious cuts and are cooked more quickly. The tenderness in stews and pot roasts does not come from using expensive cuts. It is best to use the cheaper cuts of beef, as premium beef would overcook before the meat has absorbed the flavors of the vegetables and herbs. Brisket, short ribs, and rump are the most delicious cuts for stews and pot roasts.

CHARLOTTESVILLE SHEPHERD'S PIE
[SERVES 4]

This is a favorite Virginia recipe that came straight from the English colonists—and it's a wonderful way to use leftover pot roast and stews.

$2^1/_2$ – 3 cups plain mashed potatoes
3 tablespoons butter
$1/_4$ – $1/_3$ cup milk
Salt to taste
2 eggs
2 cups finely minced leftover beef or lamb
$1/_2$ – $2/_3$ cup gravy or drippings from the leftover roast or stew
2 tablespoons chopped fresh parsley
White pepper to taste

1. Preheat the oven to 375°F.
2. Mix the mashed potatoes with 1 tablespoon of the butter, $1/_4$ cup milk, and salt to taste. Add more milk if the potatoes seem too dry. Add the eggs and beat thoroughly (but not in a food processor). Taste for salt.
3. Spread 1 cup of the potatoes on the bottom of a buttered casserole or baking dish. Cover the layer of potatoes with the meat. Add the gravy or drippings to cover well and sprinkle with the parsley. Spread the remaining potatoes on top of the meat and gravy, and dot with the remaining butter.
4. Bake, uncovered, until the potatoes are well puffed and golden brown, 25 to 30 minutes.

• To make ahead: Shepherd's Pie may be completely assembled in the morning, then refrigerated until a couple of hours before the final baking. If you take the casserole directly from the refrigerator to the oven, allow extra time for baking.

• Beef Brisket with Potatoes on the Half-Shell makes perfect leftovers for Shepherd's Pie. (see page 80)

RED WINE STEAK SAUCE

[MAKES 1 CUP]

For all beef steaks or venison steaks, or grilled hamburgers.

2   tablespoons butter

1   tablespoon chopped shallots

1   tablespoon water

1   cup dry red wine

1   clove garlic, mashed

1   teaspoon tomato paste
    Salt to taste

1   tablespoon Madeira, or more to taste

1. Melt the butter in a skillet and add the shallots and water. Cook gently until the water boils away and the shallots are tender, 2 minutes. Do not allow them to brown. 2. Add the wine and simmer for a few seconds. Then add the garlic, tomato paste, salt, and Madeira, and simmer 30 minutes. 3. Serve at the table in a sauceboat.

KENTUCKY BOURBON GRILLED STEAK

[SERVES 4 TO 6]

An interesting thing about a fine, aged Kentucky bourbon is that it tastes very much like some brandies and can often be substituted for brandy in cooking. It must, however, be an excellent bourbon, and an old one as well.

A flank steak will profit in flavor if marinated in either the Kentucky Bourbon Marinade or the Wine and Soy Marinade before grilling. Flank steak must be premium quality, or it is likely to be tough. Marinating helps to tenderize the steak, but it must be grilled quickly and sliced very thin on the bias.

1   premium flank steak, 2 to $2^{1}/_{2}$ pounds
    Good-quality vegetable or olive oil

KENTUCKY BOURBON MARINADE

1   clove garlic, cut in half

$1^{1}/_{2}$ tablespoons Kentucky bourbon

1   tablespoon vegetable oil

1   tablespoon soy sauce

1 – 2 small slivers fresh ginger or piece of dried ginger

WINE AND SOY MARINADE

$^{3}/_{4}$ cup dry white wine

$^{1}/_{2}$ cup soy sauce

2   small slivers fresh ginger or piece of dried ginger

3 – 4 scallions (green onions), chopped, or 1 clove garlic, cut in half

3   sprigs parsley

1. Remove all the excess fat and the tough membrane from the outside of the flank steak, or have the butcher do it for you.

2. Combine the ingredients for the chosen marinade in a glass, enamel, or stainless-steel pan or bowl. Place the steak in the marinade, coating it well on both sides. Allow the steak to marinate in the refrigerator for 12 to 24 hours—the longer the better. Turn the steak several times to distribute the flavors.

3. When you are ready to cook the steak, remove it from the marinade. Brush off the herbs and dry the steak well with paper towels.

4. Brush the steak with vegetable or olive oil. (The soy sauce in the marinade usually provides sufficient salt.) Broil or grill 4 inches from the heat for about 5 minutes on each side for rare steak. After the steak has been seared, brush it again with the marinade while it is cooking, if desired.

BEEF BRISKET WITH POTATOES ON THE HALF-SHELL

[SERVES 6 TO 8]

This heirloom recipe will be one of your family's favorites. Serve it with Sour Cream–Horseradish Sauce.

4 – 4^1/$_2$	pounds whole brisket
	Salt and freshly ground black pepper to taste
2	cups water, or as needed
3	sprigs fresh thyme or 1 teaspoon dried
2	bay leaves
6 – 8	Idaho potatoes, uniform size
	Watercress or parsley, for garnish
	Sour Cream–Horseradish Sauce (see sidebar)

SOUR CREAM– HORSERADISH SAUCE

1	cup sour cream
3	tablespoons prepared horseradish
	Salt to taste

Combine the ingredients in a small bowl. Transfer to a sauceboat and serve.

1. Preheat the oven to 450°F.

2. Wipe the brisket with a clean, damp cloth and season it with salt. Roast it in a deep roasting pan until golden brown, 30 to 35 minutes.

3. Add about 2 cups of water to the pan, or just enough to keep the roast from sticking and burning on the bottom. Sprinkle the roast with freshly ground pepper. Add the thyme and bay leaves. Cover, and reduce the heat to 325°F. Cook until the meat is tender, another 2 to 2^1/$_2$ hours (this will vary with the size and grade of the brisket).

4. Meanwhile, scrub the potatoes and cut them in half lengthwise.

5. About 35 to 40 minutes before the meat is done, lay the potatoes skin side up, cut side down, around the brisket. Taste the meat juices for salt. Add salt to the potatoes if needed. Allow the potatoes to cook in the meat drippings in the roasting pan. About 15 minutes before they are done, raise the heat to 425°F. Remove the cover and baste the potatoes thoroughly with the pan juices. The cut side will absorb the juices from the meat, get brown, and be delicious. Test the meat for tenderness with a thin skewer.

6. Place the brisket, whole, on a warmed platter. Surround it with the potatoes and garnish with watercress or parsley. Slice the meat only as it is served, as brisket dries out quickly. Serve with sauceboats of skimmed pan juices and Sour Cream–Horseradish Sauce.

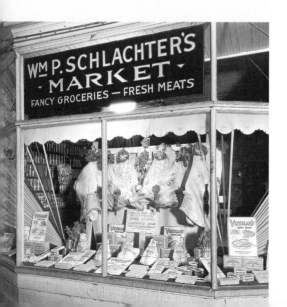

THE HUNTER'S VEAL STEW

[SERVES 4]

I was reared in the country, where we had wonderful milk-fed veal—it is still my favorite meat. Thoughts of Mother's veal roasts are warm and wonderful memories. She always made noodles to go with these veal dishes.

2	tablespoons vegetable oil
5	tablespoons butter
2	pounds veal cutlet, cut in 1^{1}/$_{2}$-inch-long julienne strips (or use veal shoulder)
	Salt and freshly ground black pepper to taste
1^{1}/$_{2}$	tablespoons finely chopped shallots
2	cups Chicken or Veal Stock, approximately (see pages 38 and 39)
1	tablespoon tomato paste, or 1 ripe tomato, peeled, seeded, or chopped
2	sprigs fresh thyme or ^{1}/$_{2}$ teaspoon dried
1	bay leaf
1^{1}/$_{2}$	teaspoons chopped fresh marjoram or ^{1}/$_{2}$ teaspoon dried
^{1}/$_{2}$	pound mushrooms, sliced
^{1}/$_{3}$	cup fresh parsley

TRIMMING

The shoulder of veal may be used instead of the cutlet, but remove all ligaments, sinews, and excess fat. Cut it into cubes. The shoulder meat will have to be cooked about 1^{1}/$_{4}$ hours longer or until very tender, but the flavor is excellent.

1. Preheat the oven to 325°F.

2. Heat the vegetable oil and 2 tablespoons of the butter in a heavy skillet. Add the veal and sauté over high heat until it is lightly browned on both sides. Season with salt and pepper. Remove the meat to a casserole with a tight-fitting cover.

3. Add the shallots to the skillet with ^{1}/$_{2}$ cup stock and cook until they are limp and the liquid has evaporated. Add the remaining stock and the tomato paste or tomato and bring to a boil. Pour this over the veal and season with the thyme, bay leaf, marjoram, and salt and pepper to taste. Cover the casserole tightly and place it in the oven. Cook for 15 minutes.

4. Meanwhile, melt the remaining butter in a medium-size skillet. Add the mushrooms and sauté them quickly over medium-high heat. Add them to the veal with their juices. Cover, and bake 20 to 25 minutes longer. Sprinkle with the parsley and serve with fresh egg noodles.

VARIATION

- Veal Stew with Wild Rice: Add 1 to 1^{1}/$_{2}$ cups cooked wild rice to the stew with the sautéed mushrooms. (Additional stock may be needed—the stew must not be dry.)

SAUCES

KENTUCKY HEIRLOOM BARBECUE SAUCE

[MAKES 1¹/₄ CUPS]

In my family's little country hotel, this was the special barbecue sauce for lamb and pork roasts—especially lamb, with which it is exquisitely compatible. In the summer a lamb barbecue with fresh corn and lima beans is pretty close to heaven.

³/₄ cup cider vinegar

²/₃ cup good-quality tomato ketchup

3 tablespoons light brown sugar

¹/₂ cup coarsely chopped onion

1 clove garlic, cut in half and cored

¹/₂ teaspoon ground ginger

2 thin lemon slices

1¹/₂ cups water

Salt and freshly ground black pepper to taste

1 tablespoon Worcestershire sauce

Tabasco sauce to taste

4 tablespoons (¹/₂ stick) unsalted butter

1. Combine the vinegar, ketchup, brown sugar, onion, garlic, ginger, lemon, and water in a stainless-steel or enamel saucepan. Bring to a boil, lower the heat, and simmer for about 25 minutes, adding a little more water if the sauce cooks too low.

2. Strain the sauce, discarding the onion, garlic, and lemon slices. Add the salt, pepper, Worcestershire, Tabasco, and butter to the strained sauce and stir well. Simmer about 5 minutes longer.

3. Set aside to ripen for 1 hour, or more if possible, before using. Keeps well under refrigeration, but freezing weakens the spices.

TALMADGE FARM BARBECUE SAUCE

[MAKES 4 CUPS]

This is a true Georgia barbecue sauce from the famous Talmadge Ham Farm in Georgia. It is the quintessential barbecue sauce of the Deep South. If that's where you grew up and you have wandered away to the North, one taste will bring tears to your eyes. I promise. Old-fashioned pit barbecues...roadside stands...summer sun beating down! The old swimming hole saved our young lives.

1 cup cider or red wine vinegar

1 tablespoon grated fresh ginger (about 2 ounces peeled)

2 tablespoons dry mustard

1¹/₄ cups good-quality ketchup

5 tablespoons Worcestershire sauce

1 clove garlic, cut in half and cored, or more to taste

1 cup light brown sugar, loosely packed

1 lemon, thinly sliced and seeded

3 tablespoons unsalted butter

Salt to taste

Lemon juice to taste

Combine the vinegar, grated ginger, mustard, ketchup, Worcestershire, garlic, brown sugar, and lemon slices in a stainless-steel or enamel saucepan. Bring to a boil, reduce the heat, and simmer 15 minutes. Add the butter and simmer 2 minutes longer. Stir in the salt and lemon juice. Set the sauce aside to ripen for several hours or overnight. (The sauce may be used as soon as it is made, but ripening improves it.) Then strain, and store it in a covered jar in the refrigerator. This will keep for several weeks, but it doesn't freeze well.

OLD SEELBACH HOUSE STEAK SAUCE

4   cups good-quality canned tomatoes,
     or 2 pounds firm ripe tomatoes, peeled

3   shallots, or 4 scallions (green onions),
     white part only

1   small clove garlic

1   cup dry red wine

1   cup red wine vinegar

2   tablespoons chopped fresh marjoram
     leaves or 1 1/2 teaspoon dried

1   tablespoon fresh thyme leaves or
     1 teaspoon dried

3   tablespoons chopped fresh parsley

1   bay leaf

1/4 cup water

1/4 cup sugar

     Salt and freshly ground black pepper
     to taste

1/4 pound mushrooms, sliced or chopped

3   tablespoons unsalted butter

1.   Combine the tomatoes and shallots or
     scallions in a blender or food processor
     and blend well. Pour into a large stainless-
     steel or enamel saucepan and simmer over
     medium heat until a thick sauce has
     formed, about 30 to 40 minutes.

2.   In the meantime, combine the garlic,
     wine, vinegar, marjoram, thyme, parsley,
     and bay leaf in a stainless-steel or enamel
     saucepan and simmer until the ingredi-
     ents have been reduced to 1/3 cup, 30
     to 40 minutes. Strain into a bowl and
     set aside.

3.   Combine the water and sugar in a heavy
     pan or skillet and cook over low heat until
     a medium-brown caramel has formed, 2 to
     3 minutes. Do not allow the sauce to become
     the least bit burned or it will be bitter.

4.   Add the wine and herb infusion to the
     caramel. Stir to blend and add the toma-
     to sauce. Add salt and pepper to taste and
     allow the flavors to ripen an hour or so
     before using; or the sauce can be made
     several days ahead and refrigerated.
     Before serving, sauté the mushrooms in
     the butter and fold them into the sauce.

VEGETABLES THAT ARE GOOD WITH BEEF

Artichokes

Broccoli

Brussels sprouts

Carrots

Cauliflower

Celeriac

Celery

Eggplant

Green beans

Kale

Leeks

Lima beans

Mushrooms

Onions

Peas

Tomatoes

Turnip greens

White potatoes

Yellow squash

Zucchini

THE WELL-DRESSED BIRDS

If we in the South had to choose only one meat for the rest of our lives, I believe the over-whelming vote would go to chicken. We can cook chicken a hundred ways and never be bored, but the topmost favorite, I think, is fried. Properly fried chicken is delicious, no doubt about it. On a restless night haven't you been delighted to find some fried chicken in the refrigerator that was left over from supper? That flavor stays in my taste memory.

If you wish to learn to cook game birds, cook chicken, lots of chicken, in various ways. Learn the difference between sautéing and frying and the change it makes in the menu. Roast, poach, and braise chickens, using different herbs. Cook and taste—taste and think.

Then transfer what you've learned from chicken to game birds, or any "wild thing" that you are fortunate enough to have often. The intricacies of the different flavors in all wild birds make them endlessly fascinating.

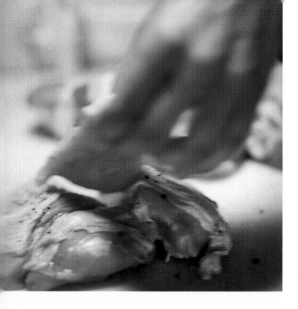

SOUTHERN FRIED CHICKEN

[SERVES 4]

Correctly fried Southern chicken is simplicity itself—and one of the best ways to cook chicken in all the world. It is never tenderized in any way before frying, nor is it steamed or braised in the oven after frying. It is not dipped in milk, crumbs, or batter—just in a generous coating of flour. Season with salt and pepper. Use fresh fat and an iron skillet. Lard makes the crispiest chicken, but vegetable shortening is fine. No bacon drippings. Serve hot or cold. Never do we have a picnic without fried chicken.

FRIED CHICKEN GRAVY

2 tablespoons drippings from
   fried chicken

2 tablespoons all-purpose flour

1¹/₂ cups milk

   Salt and freshly ground white
   pepper to taste

Pour off all the fat from the pan except about 2 tablespoons, leaving the golden brown crunchy bits. Add the flour and blend over rather low heat. Add the milk and cook, stirring constantly, until the gravy has thickened. Add salt and lots of pepper to taste. Serve over hot biscuits.

1 frying chicken, 3 to 3¹/₂ pounds
1 teaspoon salt, plus more to taste
   Freshly ground pepper to taste
1 cup all-purpose flour
   Lard or solid vegetable shortening for frying

1. Cut the chicken into comfortable serving pieces (breast cut in half, thigh and leg separated). Rinse the pieces and dry them well with paper towels. Season the chicken with salt and pepper to taste.

2. Mix 1 teaspoon salt into the flour and coat the chicken by rolling the pieces firmly in the flour or by tossing them in the flour in a plastic bag. Before frying, shake the pieces to rid them of any excess flour.

3. Heat enough lard or shortening to come to a depth of 1¹/₂ inches in a heavy black iron pan. When the fat is piping hot but not smoking, add the largest pieces first. Do not crowd. Cover the pan and fry over medium-high heat for 8 minutes.

4. After the chicken has browned on one side, turn it to brown the other side. Keep the fat at a medium-high temperature but remove the cover. (You will have to watch the chicken as it cooks.) The total cooking time for tender chicken will be about 20 minutes. Drain on paper towels.

KENTUCKY BLUEGRASS BARBECUE BASTE

[MAKES 4 CUPS]

This is a far more delicate barbecue baste and sauce than the usual Southern pit barbecues.

$^1/_2$ cup cider vinegar

1 teaspoon ground ginger, or 1 small piece (1 ounce) fresh ginger, grated or chopped

1 tablespoon dry mustard

2 tablespoons Worcestershire sauce

$^3/_4$ cup good-quality ketchup

6 tablespoons medium-dry sherry

1 bay leaf

1 clove garlic, or more to taste, cut in half and cored

2 thin lemon slices

2 tablespoons flavorless vegetable oil

6 tablespoons ($^3/_4$ stick) unsalted butter

Salt to taste

Tabasco sauce to taste

1. In a stainless-steel or enamel saucepan combine the ingredients through the oil. 2. Set aside to mellow for 1 hour, or more if possible. 3. Strain the sauce and discard the ginger (if using fresh), bay leaf, garlic, and lemon slices. Add the butter, salt, and Tabasco, and simmer for 3 minutes.

You can grate the fresh ginger by hand, or slice it and combine it with the vinegar in a food processor. Process just a few seconds. The ground ginger works quite well in this recipe, however.

BALTIMORE BARBECUE CHICKEN

[SERVES 4]

This is Maryland's way of basting chicken for the oven or grill. It is tart and spicy, but at the same time it has a delicacy unlike the tomato-rich, earthy country barbecues of the Deep South.

4 shallots or scallions (green onions; white bulb only), finely chopped

$^1/_3$ cup water

1 teaspoon dry mustard

2 tablespoons tarragon white wine vinegar

2 tablespoons good-quality ketchup

2 tablespoons lemon juice

8 tablespoons (1 stick) butter, cut into pieces and chilled

$^1/_2$ teaspoon Tabasco sauce, or to taste

Cayenne pepper to taste

Salt to taste

2 frying chickens, $2^1/_2$ to 3 pounds each, split

6 tablespoons ($^3/_4$ stick) unsalted butter; at room temperature

1. Combine the shallots or scallions with the water in a small stainless-steel or enamel saucepan and simmer until the shallots are soft, $1^1/_2$ to 2 minutes. Don't allow them to sizzle or boil dry.

2. Add the mustard, vinegar, ketchup, and lemon juice to the shallots and cook over low heat, 5 to 6 minutes. Remove from the heat and allow the flavors to ripen about 30 minutes.

3. Preheat the oven to 450°F.

4. Reheat the sauce over low heat until just warm, no hotter. Beat in the chilled butter 1 piece at a time. Add the Tabasco, cayenne, and salt. Set aside.

5. Rinse the chicken halves and dry them well with paper towels. Lay them bone side down in a large roasting pan. Season with salt, then brush with 3 tablespoons of the unsalted butter and place in the oven. Cook the chicken, basting several times with the pan drippings and the remaining butter, for 25 minutes. Allow the birds to become golden and crisp. Continue to cook, brushing the birds with the barbecue sauce several times, 6 minutes. Be careful not to let the sauce burn.

THE HERMITAGE
CHICKEN CORNBREAD SANDWICH
[SERVES 6]

The Hermitage Hotel in Nashville, Tennessee, so named for the beautiful home of Andrew Jackson, served this very Southern dish for Sunday brunch. It is actually a delicious chicken hash made without potatoes. The cornbread is at its best oven fresh, of course, but it can be made ahead and frozen, and the chicken hash holds better than it does when it is made with potatoes. The cornbread can be baked and cut into squares, or it can be made into muffins, then split and filled. Serve with your best garden relish—chow-chow, green tomato, or red and green pepper relish.

TENNESSEE
SOUR CREAM CORNBREAD

$^7/_8$	cup fine white cornmeal
1	cup sour cream
2	tablespoons milk
2	eggs
$^3/_4$	teaspoon salt
1	teaspoon sugar
$^1/_8$	teaspoon baking soda
$1^1/_2$	teaspoons baking powder
4	tablespoons ($^1/_2$ stick) butter, melted

1. Preheat the oven to 425°F. Butter a 7- or 8-inch square glass or metal cake pan. 2. Measure the cornmeal into a roomy bowl. Add the sour cream, milk, and eggs and beat thoroughly with a whisk. Add the salt, sugar, baking soda, baking powder, and melted butter. Mix thoroughly and fast. Spoon into the prepared cake pan. 3. Place the pan on the middle shelf of the oven and bake until the cornbread is golden brown, about 25 minutes. The center of the bread should be fairly firm to the touch. 4. Cut the bread into squares. Split each square horizontally, as for a sandwich. Keep warm.

	Hot Tennessee Sour Cream Cornbread (see sidebar)
2	tablespoons butter, at room temperature
3	tablespoons all-purpose flour
5	cups Rich Chicken Stock (see page 22), not quite fat-free, or more as needed
4	cups cubed freshly poached chicken (see pages 104–105)
$^1/_4$	cup chopped onion
2	cups chopped pale celery or celery hearts
	Salt and freshly ground white pepper to taste
	Cayenne pepper to taste
	Parsley springs, for garnish

1. Prepare the cornbread and keep it warm.

2. Blend the butter with the flour in a saucepan. Add 1 cup of the stock and cook over medium-low heat, stirring constantly with a whisk, until thickened and smooth, about 5 to 6 minutes. Add the chicken and shake the pan to blend.

3. Simmer the onion and celery in 4 cups stock in a large heavy pan until they are tender but retain some texture. Spoon the chicken mixture on top of the vegetables. Shake the pan to distribute the chicken lightly through the vegetables. Don't stir.

4. Add, if needed, just enough stock to make a pleasing amount of sauce for spooning the hash over the cornbread. Season with salt, white pepper, and cayenne.

5. Spoon the piping-hot chicken hash over the lower half of each cornbread square, allowing some to run over the sides. Cover with the top piece of cornbread. Garnish with a sprig of parsley and serve at once.

HERB STUFFING

[MAKES ABOUT 2 CUPS]

3   tablespoons butter

4   shallots, minced

3   slices smoked bacon, diced

2   cups finely ground fresh
    breadcrumbs

2 – 3 tablespoons chopped fresh parsley

1   teaspoon dried tarragon

$^1/_2$ cup Chicken Stock (see page 38),
    or as needed

    Salt to taste

1. Melt the butter in a large skillet over medium heat. Add the shallots and sauté until they are limp but not brown. Add the bacon and continue to cook until it has browned. 2. Add the breadcrumbs, parsley, and tarragon. Toss well with a fork. 3. Add just enough chicken stock to make a barely moist dressing, and season with salt to taste if needed.

STUFFED CORNISH GAME HENS

[SERVES 6]

Any recipe for Rock Cornish Game Hens can also be used for pheasant, partridge, chicken, or quail, but the timing will vary. Birds that have been frozen profit from a stuffing, which helps keep them moist. Baste and baste.

6   Cornish hens, ready to cook
    Herb Stuffing (see sidebar)
    Salt and freshly ground black pepper to taste

4   tablespoons ($^1/_2$ stick) butter, at room temperature

$^1/_2$ cup plus 3 tablespoons Chicken Stock (see page 38)

$^1/_4$ cup dry white wine

$1^1/_2$ teaspoons all-purpose flour

2   tablespoons Madeira or medium-dry Spanish sherry
    Watercress or parsley sprigs, for garnish

1. Preheat the oven to 450°F.

2. Rinse the game hens thoroughly and dry them well with paper towels. Fill the cavities of the game hens loosely with stuffing and truss the birds lightly. Season the hens with salt and pepper, and rub them well with butter.

3. Place the hens in a flameproof baking pan, put them in the oven, and cook, basting frequently, until they are a light golden brown, 15 to 20 minutes.

4. Lower the temperature to 350°F and continue to roast the birds until they are tender, another 30 to 40 minutes.

5. Remove the birds to a platter and keep warm. Add the $^1/_2$ cup of stock and the white wine to the pan juices, stirring to loosen all the brown bits. Blend the flour in 3 tablespoons of stock, add it to the pan, and cook until the sauce is smooth and thickened.

6. Season the sauce with Madeira or sherry, and allow it to cook a few minutes to lose the raw flavor of the wine. Pour it over the birds or serve in a sauceboat. Serve the birds garnished with watercress or parsley.

PONTCHARTRAIN TURKEY WITH OYSTERS & MUSHROOMS

[SERVES 3 TO 4]

This is an excellent way to use the dark meat of the turkey. Very delicious and appealing with the oysters and mushrooms. Serve on wild rice, on grilled cornmeal toast garnished with watercress, or serve in shallow ramekins sprinkled with chopped fresh parsley. Accompany with pickled walnuts or delicious walnut butter.

<table>
<tr><td>$^1/_2$</td><td>pint oysters</td></tr>
<tr><td>5</td><td>tablespoons butter</td></tr>
<tr><td>$1^1/_2$</td><td>cups sliced mushrooms</td></tr>
<tr><td>$1^1/_2$</td><td>tablespoons all-purpose flour</td></tr>
<tr><td>$^1/_4$</td><td>cup Chicken Stock (see page 38), or as needed</td></tr>
<tr><td>$^1/_2$</td><td>cup heavy or whipping cream</td></tr>
<tr><td>$1^1/_2$</td><td>cups cubed cooked dark meat of turkey (One pound of cooked turkey removed from the bone equals 3 cups cubed.)</td></tr>
</table>

Salt and freshly ground black pepper to taste

1. Drain the oysters and reserve the liquor. Melt 1 tablespoon of the butter in a small saucepan. Add the oysters and cook just until the edges begin to curl, 2 minutes. Set aside.

2. Melt $1^1/_2$ tablespoons of the butter in a medium-size skillet over medium-high heat. Add the mushrooms and sauté until they absorb some of the butter but are still crisp, 2 to 3 minutes. (They must not brown.) Set aside.

3. Melt the remaining butter in a saucepan. Add the flour and blend, stirring until it is smooth. Combine the oyster liquid and enough chicken stock to make $^1/_2$ cup. Whisk it into the butter mixture. Whisk in the cream and simmer until the sauce thickens, 2 to 3 minutes.

4. Add the oysters, turkey, and mushrooms to the sauce. Season with salt and pepper to taste. Simmer until heated through, 5 minutes.

VARIATIONS

*   It is delicious and most appealing to add 3 dried black Chinese mushrooms that have been revived in water, slivered, and cooked with the sauce. That touch of black! And the flavor!
*   It is not amiss to add 1 tablespoon of Madeira or medium-dry sherry to the sauce and allow it to cook for a minute or so to mellow.

VEGETABLES THAT ARE GOOD WITH POULTRY

Artichokes

Asparagus

Broccoli

Carrots

Cauliflower

Celeriac

Celery

Eggplant

Green beans

Lima beans

Mushrooms

Onions

Peas

Potatoes, white and sweet

Tomatoes

Yellow squash

Zucchini

TO COOK CHESTNUTS

1. Preheat the oven to 425°F. 2. With a sharp knife, cut a cross or 2 gashes in the flat side of each chestnut. Put the nuts in a baking pan and roast in the oven for 10 minutes. Remove the pan and reduce the heat to 375°F. 3. Cool the chestnuts, then remove the shells and inner brown skin. Put the peeled chestnuts in a saucepan with 2 cups of the stock. Add a pinch of salt, the 1 tablespoon of sugar, and 2 tablespoons of the butter. Cover, bring to a boil, and simmer until tender, 10 to 15 minutes. Drain and set aside.

ROAST PHEASANT WITH APPLES & CHESTNUTS

[SERVES 4]

A gorgeous and festive bird for the holidays or to celebrate the hunter's bag.

2	pounds large chestnuts, cooked (see sidebar)
2²/₃	cups Veal or Chicken Stock (see pages 38 and 39)
	Salt to taste
¹/₂	cup plus 1 tablespoon sugar
4	tablespoons (1/2 stick) butter, or more as needed
1	large young pheasant, 3 pounds, ready to cook
	Freshly ground black pepper to taste
9	tart apples, such as Winesap
1	rib celery, broken in half
¹/₄	small onion
¹/₂	teaspoon crushed dried rosemary
2	slices salt pork or smoked bacon
¹/₃	cup dry Madeira or Spanish sherry
	Juice of 1 lemon
³/₄	cup water
	Watercress sprigs, for garnish

1. Preheat the oven to 375°F.

2. Rinse the pheasant thoroughly and dry it well with paper towels. Season the cavity with salt and pepper. Peel 1 apple and put it and the celery, onion, and rosemary in the cavity. Sew the opening closed and cover the pheasant with the salt pork or bacon. Secure the legs and wings with string.

3. Place the pheasant in a flameproof roasting pan and cook in the oven, basting the bird often with the butter, 30 minutes. Pour the Madeira or sherry into the pan and continue to baste until the pheasant is tender, about 15 minutes more.

4. While the bird is roasting, prepare the apples: Peel and core the remaining apples and put them in a flameproof baking dish. Combine the lemon juice and water, and pour this over the apples. Cook on top of the stove over low heat or in the 375°F oven, basting the apples often with the lemon water. Add the ¹/₂ cup sugar as needed if the apples are too tart. Continue basting until the apples are transparent and tender but not mushy. Sprinkle the tops of the apples with a little sugar and run them under the broiler to glaze a bit. Set aside and keep warm.

5. Remove the pheasant to a warm platter. Discard the salt pork or bacon.

6. Add the remaining stock to the pan and loosen the brown crusty bits from the bottom of the pan over medium-high heat. Taste, and correct the seasonings if needed. Pour the hot sauce over the pheasant, surround it with the chestnuts and apples, and garnish with watercress.

BRUNSWICK STEW

Brunswick Stew is a hearty, thick game and vegetable dish, somewhere between a soup and a stew, and eaten with a spoon. It has a touch of red pepper but no Worcestershire sauce. It is not a burgoo. It is believed to have been created first in Brunswick County, Virginia, but it is well known all through the good ham country of the South. The vegetables in a traditional Brunswick stew are tomatoes, onions, celery, carrots, potatoes, lima beans, and corn, with the emphasis on the lima beans and corn. Any delicate game, such as squab or pheasant or dove, is admissible, but the ham bone is a necessity. If you can only get chicken and ham, you can still have a delicious Brunswick Stew.

BRUNSWICK STEW

[SERVES 15 TO 18]

When the farmers or hunters brought a squirrel and rabbits to our hotel kitchen door, we knew we would have Brunswick Stew next day, and we loved it. Serve with corn muffins.

1	baked ham bone, from a Virginia or other good-quality country-cured ham if possible
6	quarts water, or as needed
1	stewing hen or 2 fryer chickens, 5 pounds total, split
1	young rabbit, $2^1/_2$ pounds, ready to cook and cut into 4 pieces
1	small young squirrel, $1^1/_2$ pounds, ready to cook and cut into 4 pieces
2	bay leaves
1	teaspoon dried thyme or several sprigs fresh
4	sprigs parsley
2	ribs celery, cut in half
2	small onions
	Several black peppercorns
4	cups tomatoes, fresh or canned, peeled and chopped
$1^1/_2$	cups peeled carrots, chopped
2	cups chopped celery
$1^1/_2$	cups chopped onions
3	large or 4 small mealy potatoes (Idaho or russet), cubed
2	cups lima beans, fresh if possible, or home frozen
3	cups corn, fresh if possible, or frozen
$1/_2$	crushed dried red chile pepper, or 1 fresh chile pepper, chopped
	Salt and freshly ground black pepper to taste

1. Put the ham bone in a large kettle with the water, bring to a boil, reduce the heat, and simmer 1 hour. Let the stock cool down a bit.

2. Rinse the hen or chickens, the rabbit, and the squirrel thoroughly and dry them well with paper towels. Add the hen or chickens to the kettle. (Use the giblets for another purpose or discard them.) Add the rabbit, squirrel, bay leaves, thyme, parsley, halved celery ribs, whole onions, and the peppercorns. Simmer, uncovered, until the chickens, squirrel, and rabbit are thoroughly tender, $1^3/_4$ hours.

3. Remove the ham bone, chickens, squirrel, and rabbit. Cover the meat and set it aside. Strain the stock and discard the seasoning vegetables and herbs. Skim some of the fat from the stock.

4. Add the tomatoes, carrots, celery, onions, potatoes, lima beans, corn, and red chile pepper. Simmer, uncovered, until all the vegetables are tender, 4 minutes.

5. Bone the chicken, rabbit, and squirrel, and remove any pieces of ham (free of fat) from the ham bone. Return the meat to the kettle. Add more water if needed to make a thick soup. Simmer for 10 to 15 minutes to let the flavors ripen and season with salt and freshly ground pepper.

COLONEL HAMBY'S
BARBECUED HAUNCH OF VENISON

[SERVES 3 PEOPLE PER POUND]

My brother, Colonel Henry Gordon Hamby, of Williamsburg, Virginia, a real gourmet who has eaten all over the world, says that he doesn't cook a haunch of venison every day but when he does, this is the way he cooks it. A haunch of venison consists of the leg (without the shank), the rump, and the loin— a colossal piece of meat—but a smaller roast can be prepared by this same method.

VEGETABLES THAT ARE GOOD WITH GAME

Carrots

Celeriac

Chestnuts

Frenched Green Beans

Lentils

Mushrooms

Onions

Rice, wild and brown

Spinach

Turnips (for duck)

Watercress

White potatoes

Top-Secret Barbecue Sauce (see page 105)

1   small haunch of young deer (10 to 12 pounds), ready to cook

Salt to taste

1. Make the barbecue sauce and set it aside.

2. Preheat the oven to 425°F.

3. Place the venison on a rack in a roasting pan and season it with salt. Roast the meat in the oven until golden brown, about 30 to 35 minutes.

4. Reduce the heat to 350°F and baste the meat thoroughly with the barbecue sauce. Continue to baste often as the venison cooks. The roasting time is the same as for beef and can be calculated in the same way; a quick-reading meat thermometer inserted in the thickest part should register 125°F for rare or 140°F for well done.

5. Allow the roast to rest for 15 to 20 minutes before carving. Brush the roast again with the sauce just before carving.

VARIATION

• Spit-Roasted Barbecued Venison: Spit the roast and cook over medium-hot coals until golden brown. Then baste with the barbecue sauce often and continue to roast over low but constant coals until the desired temperature is reached on a quick-reading meat thermometer.

POULTRY

HOW TO ROAST A PERFECT CHICKEN

[SERVES 4]

A glistening, golden brown roasted chicken that is succulent and moist is a thing of beauty and flavor—well worth your tender, loving care. Baste with pure butter and keep basting! This prevents the skin from drying out and seals in the natural juices. When a meat thermometer inserted into the thigh registers 180°F, the chicken is done. A meat thermometer is a valuable tool to a good cook.

Serve roast chicken with boiled new or small potatoes and stuffed zucchini, using fresh herbs when available.

1	fresh roasting chicken, 4 to 4¹/₂ pounds
1	lemon, cut in half
	Salt and freshly ground white pepper to taste
8	tablespoons (1 stick) butter, or more as needed, at room temperature
1	cup Rich Chicken Stock (see page 22)
1	tablespoon chopped fresh parsley
	Watercress or parsley, for garnish

1. Preheat the oven to 425°F.
2. Rinse and clean the chicken well, removing any innards that cling to the cavity. Pat dry with paper towels, then rub the cavity of the chicken with the lemon and sprinkle with salt.
3. Blend the butter with salt and white pepper to taste, and rub it all over the chicken.
4. Put the chicken, breast side up, on a rack in a fairly shallow pan and roast until golden brown, 30 minutes.
5. Turn the chicken on one side and baste with pan drippings and some of the remaining butter. Lower the heat to 325°F and cook the chicken until the exposed skin is golden brown, about 20 minutes. Baste the bird several times. Sprinkle with pepper if desired.
6. Turn the chicken on the other side. Brush well with butter. Continue to cook until the second side is golden brown, another 20 minutes. Sprinkle with pepper if desired, and baste with the pan drippings several times.
7. Lay the chicken on its back. If you own a meat thermometer, use it to test for doneness (see headnote) or plunge a skewer into the thick part of a thigh. If the juices run perfectly clear, the chicken is done. Place the chicken on a hot platter and keep warm. Allow the chicken to rest 15 minutes for easier carving.
8. Meanwhile, drain off all the fat from the pan and add the stock, scraping the browned bits and glaze from the bottom of the pan. Allow the stock to boil for a few minutes. Season with parsley, and salt if needed.
9. Serve the sauce in a sauceboat alongside the chicken. Garnish the platter with bouquets of watercress or parsley.

HOW TO POACH CHICKEN BREASTS

1. Rinse 3 whole chicken breasts and dry them well with paper towels. Cut the breasts in half. Remove the wing tip, if the wing is attached, but not the wing bone.
2. Put the breasts in a tight-fitting kettle or enamel Dutch oven. Cover with fresh, cold, fat-free chicken stock or water, using as much chicken stock as you can spare, but at least half. Add 2 ribs of cel-

ery cut into pieces, 1 medium onion, 1 bay leaf, and a pinch of dried thyme. Taste the broth for salt, then add salt accordingly. Breasts must cook in lightly salted stock.

3. Bring the liquid to a boil, reduce the heat, cover loosely, and simmer only until the breasts are tender, about 20 minutes. Overcooking makes the meat dry.

4. Uncover the pot and let the chicken cool in the stock. Remove the meat from the bones. Use for salad, hash, curry, and sandwiches.

HERBS THAT ARE OUTSTANDING IN STEWS

- Parsley is of time-honored importance to the good cook. It lends a needed freshness to winter stews, and it is the greatest companion of all to the potato.

- Rosemary is a beautiful name and a charming herb. It does wonders for all kinds of stews—lamb, chicken, and especially pork. Its fragrance is stronger when fresh than when dried.

- Sweet Marjoram: A sprig of fresh marjoram is a delight to our sense of smell. It almost tells you where to use it—chicken and pasta, lamb dishes, and the herb bouquet. I never seem to plant enough.

- Tarragon: It is said that tarragon is the herb of the gourmet. It does have a style all its own. Tarragon seems to elevate each dish it flavors. It is not a country herb—far from it. Tarragon is not as indispensable as thyme, but used in the appropriate dish, such as chicken or veal, it is exquisitely pleasing.

- Thyme and Bay Leaf are two herbs that enhance each other and work their magic in meat and seafood stews. Make a fine stew without them? It can't be done. But use the dried imported bay leaf, as the American bay leaves do not have the authentic flavor.

CHECKPOINTS FOR POULTRY

- 3 pounds of dressed poultry yields approximately 1 pound cooked meat.

- A 4$^{1}/_{2}$- to 5-pound hen yields 1$^{1}/_{4}$ pounds meat.

- 1 pound of cooked poultry meat yields 3 cups cubed.

- Poultry for salad or hash should be poached, not baked.

- Allow freshly cooked fowl or broth to cool to room temperature before refrigerating.

- Never cover hot fowl or stock.

- Chicken stock freezes well for a long period.

- Chervil, parsley, marjoram, and tarragon are herbs that are compatible with poultry.

TOP-SECRET BARBECUE SAUCE

This unusual barbecue sauce contains no tomato. An old soldier gave this recipe to my brother during World War II. He was sworn to secrecy, but after all these years we think it should be shared.

The basting sauce is at its best with lamb or a haunch of venison. Work with it yourself and discover its hidden magic and the ways you like to use it.

$^{1}/_{2}$ cup cider vinegar

1$^{1}/_{2}$ cups water

1 teaspoon dry mustard

$^{1}/_{4}$ teaspoon cayenne pepper, or more to taste

1 teaspoon Hungarian paprika

2 tablespoons sugar

2 teaspoons salt

1 tablespoon Worcestershire sauce

1 tablespoon Tabasco sauce

1 tablespoon chili powder

1 tablespoon freshly ground black pepper

Juice of $^{1}/_{2}$ lemon

1 medium onion, coarsely chopped

1 clove garlic, crushed or sliced, or more to taste

8 tablespoons (1 stick) unsalted butter

1. Combine all the ingredients except the butter in a stainless-steel or enamel pan. Bring to a boil, reduce the heat, and simmer 15 minutes. Remove the pan from heat and allow the flavors to ripen 30 minutes.

2. Strain the sauce into another pan and add the butter. Bring to a simmer again and cook until the butter melts. Mix well and remove from the heat. This sauce keeps well under refrigeration, but don't freeze it.

- Watch the sauce carefully so it does not burn. If at any time it begins to cook too low, add a small amount of water.

A FINE KETTLE OF FISH

Take a quick glance at a map of the United States, following the Chesapeake Bay in Maryland to the Florida Keys, and you will see why Southerners have an embarrassment of riches in fish and seafood. The waters adjoining the land provide crabmeat, crawfish, shrimp, oysters, scallops, clams, the great family of snappers, pompano, and redfish—the list goes on and on, with all the mollusks, crustaceans, and fish one's heart could desire.

Another glance at our inland states, such as Kentucky and Tennessee, shows the blue of lakes and rivers that deliver a bountiful larder of freshwater fish—bass, crappie, walleyed pike, catfish, bluegills, and salmon trout. This list, too, goes on and on.

In the pages that follow you will find my favorite fish and seafood recipes gleaned from 50 years of cooking and tasting—and loving it. Give me a fresh fish with some butter, salt and pepper, and lemon juice, a few boiled new potatoes with a bouquet of herbs from the garden, a little green salad, some good bread, and chilled white wine, and we shall dine tonight.

FRENCH-FRIED FINGERS OF FLOUNDER

[SERVES 4]

In New Orleans these small pieces of fried flounder are called "goujonettes." A goujon is a coupling bolt or a link-pin on a bicycle, and these small, curly pieces of fish are shaped somewhat like one. Hot, crunchy goujonettes—and french-fried potatoes. I think I shall make homemade mayonnaise for the tartar sauce—it will be simply delicious with the fresh dill I found at the market today.

$2^{1}/_{4}$ pounds flounder fillets

    Salt to taste

1   cup all-purpose flour

2   eggs

$^{1}/_{3}$ cup milk

3   cups fresh breadcrumbs

    Solid vegetable shortening or oil for deep-frying

    Freshly ground black pepper to taste

    Sprigs of watercress or parsley, for garnish

    Lemon wedges, for garnish

    Tartar Sauce with Dill (see sidebar)

1. Dry the fillets well and cut them into diagonal strips about $^{1}/_{2}$ inch wide. Season with salt. Roll each piece of fish in flour.

2. Beat the eggs and milk in a bowl until well mixed. Shake off any excess flour and dip the fish fingers into the egg mixture, then roll them in the crumbs, pressing hard so the crumbs will stick. (This can be done a few hours ahead if desired.)

3. Add shortening or oil, 3 inches deep or more, to a heavy deep skillet or pan, and heat to 370°F on a deep-fat thermometer. The shortening or oil will ripple in the pan when ready. Do not allow it to smoke or the fish will cook so fast on the outside that the inside won't have a chance to get done.

4. Drop the fish fingers into the hot fat a few at a time and fry only until golden brown, about 2 to 3 minutes. Drain at once on paper towels. Sprinkle with salt and pepper and serve garnished with watercress or parsley, and lemon wedges and tartar sauce on the side.

•   Accompany the fish with french-fried potatoes and Country Garden Slaw.

TARTAR SAUCE WITH DILL

[MAKES ABOUT $1^{1}/_{4}$ CUPS]

To serve with fried fish or shellfish.

3   tablespoons fresh onion juice (see step 1)

1   cup Blender Mayonnaise (see page 61)

2   tablespoons finely chopped dill pickle

2   teaspoons fresh lemon juice

$1^{1}/_{2}$ tablespoons chopped fresh dill

1. Prepare the onion juice by straining a grated onion through cheesecloth to extract the liquid. 2. Combine and blend all the ingredients. Place in a closed jar and refrigerate.

VARIATION

Tartar Sauce with Capers: Omit the dill pickle and fresh dill. Add 2 tablespoons drained capers and 3 tablespoons chopped fresh parsley.

One onion peeled and cut in half can be marinated in the sauce for several hours, then discarded. Omit the onion juice.

FLORIDA SOLE & SCALLOPS WITH SAFFRON

[SERVES 4]

The Spanish left a notable trademark Florida cookery with their saffron. It is a luxurious spice now—but still unique, delicious, and beautiful. Splurge.

4   tablespoons ($\frac{1}{2}$ stick) butter
2   tablespoons all-purpose flour
1$\frac{3}{4}$ cups well-flavored Fish or Veal Stock (see pages 38 and 39)
      A few threads of Florida saffron or $\frac{1}{2}$ teaspoon powdered saffron
$\frac{1}{2}$ cup heavy or whipping cream
      Salt and freshly ground white pepper to taste
      Cayenne pepper to taste
$\frac{1}{2}$ pound scallops
1   pound lemon sole fillets
      Chopped fresh parsley, for garnish

1. Preheat the oven to 375°F.
2. Melt 2 tablespoons of the butter in a heavy saucepan or in a double boiler over simmering water. Add the flour and blend well. Stir until smooth, about 1 minute. (Do not allow the flour to brown.)
3. Gradually add 1$\frac{1}{4}$ cups of the stock and the saffron. Beat well with a whisk until the sauce has thickened and has turned a lovely shade of yellow.
4. Add the cream, season with salt, white pepper, and cayenne, and cook over medium-low heat for a few minutes to thicken. Set aside but keep warm.
5. Cut the scallops in half if they are large. Put the sole and scallops in a shallow baking dish. Season with salt. Pour the remaining stock over the seafood and cover lightly with foil.
6. Bake in the oven until the sole flakes easily with a fork, 5 to 6 minutes.
7. Gently pour off the liquid. Pour saffron cream sauce over the sole and scallops. Dot with the remaining butter. Return to the oven to heat only until bubbly and just beginning to brown, 2 minutes. Sprinkle with parsley and serve immediately.

•   Any fresh sole, Northern or Southern, as well as any kind of scallops can be used in this dish.

SAINTLY SCALLOPS

Scallop shells are considered by artists to be one of the most beautiful designs in nature, and the scallop is most certainly one of our most delicious seafoods.

In France, scallops are always called Coquilles Saint-Jacques, or St. James shells, a name that goes back to the Middle Ages. According to legend, Saint James the Great, after his martyrdom in Judea, was set adrift at sea but was safely guided by the angels to the shores of Padrón, in Spain.

In the twelfth century, a cathedral was erected over St. James's grave at Santiago de Compostela, and this soon became a shrine for French pilgrims, who crossed the Pyrenees into Spain.

GREEN MAYO

3 tablespoons chopped fresh parsley

1 tablespoon chopped chives

1½ tablespoons chopped
   fresh tarragon

2 cups homemade mayonnaise
   (see page 60)

   Fresh lemon juice to taste

Fold the herbs into the mayonnaise
and season with lemon juice to taste.
Allow to stand an hour or so in the
refrigerator to ripen before using.
Serve with cold salmon, hard-cooked
eggs, and a variety of seafood hors
d'oeuvres.

POMPANO EN PAPILLOTE

[SERVES 8]

The most highly esteemed fish that swims from the Carolinas to Florida is the silver pompano—
fine-grained, delicate, and delectable, but fragile. It must be eaten very fresh from the water. Pompano
ages rapidly; it does not withstand shipping or idling too long in the refrigerator. I used to meet the boats
in Florida as they came in late in the afternoon—and then sauté, broil, or bake the fish for supper.
For company, it's fun to do Pompano en Papillote—elegant but easy.

8   whole small pompano (as uniform in size as possible), ¾ to 1 pound each

     Juice of 2 lemons, or more as needed

     Salt to taste

8   tablespoons (1 stick) butter, or more as needed, at room temperature

3   shallots, minced

½   pound mushrooms, chopped

2   slices canned pimiento, chopped

     Freshly ground white pepper to taste

     Chopped fresh parsley, or a mixture of parsley and tarragon, for garnish

     Watercress sprigs, for garnish

     Lemon wedges, for garnish

1.   Cut aluminum foil or cooking parchment into 8 heart-shaped pieces large enough to enclose the fish.

2.   Clean and gut each fish, leaving the head and tail intact (or discard the head if you wish). Dry them
     well with paper towels. Season the cavity of each fish with lemon juice and salt. Set aside.

3.   Melt 4 tablespoons of the butter in a skillet and gently sauté the shallots and mushrooms, so that
     the shallots cook in the juice of the mushrooms and do not sizzle. Add the chopped pimiento and
     a little lemon juice (this enhances the flavor of the mushrooms). Set aside to cool.

4.   Preheat the oven to 425°F.

5.   Spread the remaining butter generously over the fish and season with salt and white pepper. Lay
     the fish on one side of each piece of foil. Put a tablespoon or so of the mushroom filling on top
     of each fish, followed by a sprinkling of parsley or herb mixture. Fold the foil over the fish and
     crimp the edges together.

6.   Arrange the fish packets on a pastry sheet and place them in the oven. Bake 5 to 6 minutes plus
     10 minutes per inch of thickness of the fish. Use one fish (yours) as a test—if it flakes easily when
     touched with a fork, it's done.

7.   Serve each pompano in its packet, opened a bit and steaming hot, with a cluster of watercress and
     a wedge of lemon by its side.

TROUT A LA MARGUERY

[SERVES 6]

This is a very old and famous dish from New Orleans, but it was created at Marguery's restaurant in Paris in the late nineteenth century. In the New Orleans restaurants they usually make a hollandaise sauce and let it go at that, but the original Trout Marguery was made the way it is given here. It is a rich dish, but that can be balanced nicely with a light menu, so it need not be overpowering.

1	pound white-fleshed fish, such as grouper or sole
$3/4$ – 1	pound extra fish bones
2	carrots, peeled and sliced
1	medium onion, cut into quarters
4	sprigs parsley
8	peppercorns
1	bay leaf
3	slices lemon
2	quarts water
6	small trout, about 6 ounces each, cleaned and gutted
5	tablespoons butter, melted
	Salt to taste
	Cayenne pepper to taste
$1/3$	cup dry white wine
8	tablespoons (1 stick) butter, chilled
3	egg yolks, at room temperature
	Squeeze of lemon juice, or to taste
24	small shrimp, shelled and deveined
25	shucked small oysters
	Lemon wedges, for garnish
	Fresh parsley or watercress sprigs, for garnish

FISH THAT ARE GOOD FOR GRILLING AND BROILING

Bass

Black striped bass (rockfish)

Cod

Crappie

Flounder

Freshwater bass

Grouper

Mackerel

Pompano

Porgy

Redfish

Red snapper

Scrod

Sole

Salmon trout

Swordfish

Trout

1. Put the white-fleshed fish and bones in a large saucepan. Add the carrots, onion, parsley, peppercorns, bay leaf, lemon slices, and water. Bring to a boil and cook until the liquid is reduced to 2 cups, 15 to 25 minutes depending on the pan's shape. Strain through a fine sieve into another saucepan and discard the bones and fish. Reduce the strained stock to about $1/3$ cup, 8 minutes.
2. Dry the trout with paper towels.
3. Lay the trout in a generously buttered baking dish. Brush them well with the melted butter and season with salt and cayenne pepper.
4. Preheat the oven to 375°F. Uncover the trout and bake until the fish flakes easily when touched with a fork, 15 to 18 minutes. (Allow about 10 minutes per inch of thickness of the fish.)

5. While the fish is cooking, put the reduced stock and the white wine in a double boiler over simmering water. Add the chilled butter a little at a time, beating it in until the sauce thickens. Don't allow the sauce to get too hot or it will not thicken. Beat in the egg yolks slowly. Do not allow the sauce to become too hot or the yolks will harden. Season to taste with salt, cayenne, and lemon juice.

6. Add the shrimp and oysters to the hot butter sauce around the trout. Return the pan to the oven just long enough to cook the seafood (the edges of the oysters will curl).

7. Lift the trout onto a warmed ovenproof platter, and raise the oven heat to 500°F. Place the shrimp and oysters around the trout. Spoon the sauce over the shrimp and oysters. Add some of the liquid from the trout if there isn't enough sauce to cover. This dish must not be dry.

8. Place the platter in the oven (or run it under the broiler) just long enough for the dish to heat thoroughly, about 1 minute. Watch it carefully or the sauce will curdle.

9. Garnish with wedges of lemon and clusters of parsley or watercress.

Grouper and sole are especially good for making fish stock, as they are rich in gelatin. The fish stock can be made ahead and strained (step 1) and then refrigerated, if desired.

CRAYFISH

Crayfish, or crawfish as they are called in Louisiana, are freshwater crustaceans, and so delicate and sweet that hundreds of gastronomes have made the journey to New Orleans just to eat them. *Etouffée* means "smothered" in French, and it became a Creole term for crawfish smothered in their own juices and butter, and seasoned with red peppers—cayenne, red bell pepper, and paprika. The great charm of a good Crawfish Etouffee is that the unique flavor of the fish is honored and is not disguised by an armada of ersatz powders and non-essential seasonings.

CRAWFISH ETOUFFÉE

[SERVES 4]

Traditionally, Crawfish Etouffée was served with rice, but it is never mixed with rice. Now it is often served around pasta.

3	cups peeled cooked crawfish tails (see page 129)
$^1/_2$	cup finely chopped onions
$^1/_2$	cup finely chopped scallions (green onions) or shallots
$^1/_4$	cup finely chopped green bell pepper
$^3/_4$	cup finely chopped red bell pepper
$^3/_4$	cup ($1^1/_2$ sticks) unsalted butter, chilled
1	cup crawfish bouillon (see page 129) or Fish Stock (see page 38) or water
1	large ripe firm tomato, peeled, seeded, and chopped
1	teaspoon Hungarian paprika
$^1/_2$	teaspoon cayenne pepper, or to taste
$^1/_2$	teaspoon salt, or to taste
4	cups freshly cooked white rice or pasta, such as thin linguine (see page 152)
	Watercress, for garnish
8	cooked whole crawfish tails, for garnish

1. Prepare the crawfish and set aside.
2. Combine the onions, scallions or shallots, green and red bell peppers, 2 tablespoons of the butter, and $^1/_4$ cup of the bouillon, stock, or water in a large non-aluminum skillet or saucepan. Simmer over medium heat until the onions are limp and the stock has boiled away, about 5 minutes. Do not allow the onions to sizzle or brown the least bit.
3. Add the tomato and remaining $^3/_4$ cup bouillon, stock, or water. Continue simmering until the peppers, onions, and tomato are soft, about 20 minutes. Do not allow this to boil. Add the paprika, cayenne, and about $^1/_2$ teaspoon salt. Stir to blend.
4. Add the remaining butter, 1 tablespoon at a time, keeping the pan over low heat and stirring constantly with a wooden spoon. Always stir in one direction so the sauce will become homogenized and thicken.
5. When all the butter has been added, toss in the crawfish. Continue to stir in the same direction, allowing the crawfish to blend with the sauce, but do not overcook. (The sauce should look as if heavy cream has been added.) Taste for salt and cayenne, and add more if desired.
6. Mound hot rice or pasta on warmed plates. Surround with the blushing pink crawfish in its delectable sauce.
7. Place a few sprigs of watercress on each plate and a cooked red crawfish tail on either side of the watercress.

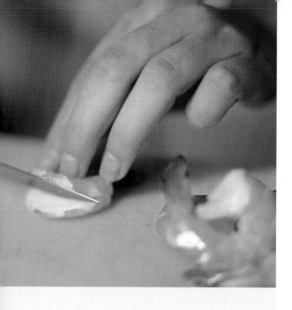

JAMBALAYA SAUCE WITH PASTA

This flavorful sauce, especially when made with country ham, is delightful served over hot noodles. Follow directions for Jambalaya, but omit the rice and shrimp. It is not traditional, but 1 slivered red bell pepper is a good addition.

JAMBALAYA

[SERVES 4]

Jambalaya originated with the Spanish when they came to Louisiana in the late 1700s. It is a direct descendant of their paella, but in the New World it became known as a Creole dish—and a delicious one.

2	tablespoons lard or solid vegetable shortening
6	ounces unbaked country smoked ham or any good smoked ham, cut into $^1/_2$-inch slivers
3	slices smoked bacon
$^1/_2$	cup chopped onion
1	large can (28 ounces) tomatoes, or $3^1/_2$ cups peeled fresh ripe tomatoes plus 1 cup fresh tomato juice
2	ribs celery, cut in half
2	bay leaves
4	sprigs thyme or 1 teaspoon dried
4	large sprigs parsley
1	fresh small red chile pepper, sliced, or $^1/_2$ dried, crumbled, or to taste
$^1/_4$	teaspoon ground cumin, or to taste
1	clove garlic, unpeeled
	Salt to taste
1	cup long-grain rice
3	cups Chicken or Veal Stock (see pages 38 and 39), or more as needed
$1^1/_2$	pounds small shrimp, shelled, deveined, and refrigerated
	Chopped fresh parsley, for garnish

1. Heat the lard or shortening in a large heavy pan or Dutch oven. Add the ham and sauté lightly, but do not fry or allow it to become brown.

2. Add the bacon, onion, tomatoes with their juice, celery, bay leaves, thyme, parsley, chile pepper, and cumin. Stick the garlic with a toothpick (for easy removal) and add it. Bring to a boil, reduce the heat, and simmer for about 1 hour. If the sauce boils too low, add a little of the stock. Season with salt.

3. When the sauce has developed a good flavor, add the rice and 3 cups stock. Toss thoroughly with a fork. Cover the pan and simmer over low heat (or bake in a 350°F oven) until the rice is almost tender, about 1 hour, adding more stock if the mixture becomes too dry. It must remain moist and almost creamy. You may have to place it over a "flame-tamer" to prevent it from sticking.

4. Five minutes before the dish is done, remove the bacon, celery, bay leaves, sprigs of thyme, parsley, and garlic. Season with salt if needed. Add the shrimp and toss them through the rice with a fork. Add a little stock if it is needed. Simmer just long enough for the shrimp to cook, 3 to 4 minutes. (The time depends on the size of the shrimp; they will toughen if overcooked.) Sprinkle with chopped parsley and serve.

SAUTÉED SOFT-SHELL CRABS

[SERVES 3]

The simplest way of all is the best way to cook soft-shell crabs. Their flavor is that delicate and that evanescent. Don't even dip them in beaten egg—that too masks their flavor. Dust them with flour, then sauté in butter and season with salt, freshly ground white pepper, and lemon juice. Serve with new potatoes, tiny green beans, peas, or asparagus with a light hollandaise. Add homemade hot rolls and frozen chocolate soufflé. Live.

HOW TO DRESS SOFT-SHELL CRABS

Cook soft-shell crabs as soon as possible after they have been dressed. If you have to buy the crabs the day before using, have the fishmonger pack them alive in seaweed or grass. Refrigerate them, then dress shortly before using.

1. Select crabs that are alive and "wiggling." 2. Snip off the eyes with scissors. This brings instant and painless death. 3. Turn the crab on its back and remove the apron. Lift up the flaps at each end and pull out the spongy gill tissue. 4. Press above the legs and pull out the sac. Clean the crabs well under cold running water. 5. Pat the crabs dry with paper towels.

6	small soft-shell crabs, dressed
	Salt to taste
6	tablespoons all-purpose flour, or as needed
8	tablespoons (1 stick) unsalted butter
	Freshly ground white pepper to taste
	Fresh lemon juice to taste
	Watercress sprigs, for garnish
	Lemon wedges, for garnish

1. Dry the crabs well, sprinkle them with salt, and dust lightly with the flour. Do not dredge or coat the crabs too heavily.

2. Melt the butter in a heavy skillet over medium-high heat. (I am partial to my heavy copper skillet, but black iron is fine.) Sauté the crabs (do not crowd them) in the foaming butter until golden brown on one side, then turn to brown the other side. Turn them only once, about 3 to 5 minutes on each side. The crabs, like almost all fish and shellfish, should not be cooked fast, but the butter must not burn or turn very dark.

3. Sprinkle the crabs again with a little salt, and season with white pepper and a squeeze or two of lemon juice. Spoon the lovely golden butter in the skillet over the crabs, and serve garnished with watercress and lemon wedges.

VARIATIONS

*   Add 1½ teaspoons buttered and toasted sliced or slivered almonds per crab at serving time.
*   Add a sprinkling of chopped fresh herbs, such as dill and parsley, or tarragon and parsley, or chervil and parsley. Chervil possibly is the best.
*   A few capers that have been marinated in tarragon vinegar are delicious when added with the sprinkling of lemon juice.

MARYLAND CRAB CAKES

[SERVES 4]

These Maryland crab cakes are considered to be very fine. They do not have onions or shallots, as many do.

1	pound fresh lump crabmeat
	Juice of $^1/_2$ lemon
2	tablespoons butter
2	tablespoons all-purpose flour
$^1/_2$	cup milk
$^1/_4$	teaspoon dry mustard
2	egg yolks, at room temperature
1	tablespoon capers, or more to taste, drained
	Salt and freshly ground white pepper to taste
	Cayenne pepper to taste
6	tablespoons ($^3/_4$ stick) unsalted butter
2	tablespoons vegetable oil
	Lemon wedges, for garnish
	Homemade mayonnaise (see page 60), for garnish

COATING

$1^1/_4$	cups fresh breadcrumbs (see step 4)
$^1/_2$	cup all-purpose flour
1	egg
$^1/_3$	cup milk

BEAUTIFUL SWIMMER

Contrary to the belief of many, the blue crab and the so-called soft-shell crab are the same species (*Callinectes sapidus*). The sapidus crab (*sapidus* means savory and tasteful) is found in the U.S. from the Delaware Bay down to Florida and the Gulf states. The crabs shed their hard coats many times before maturity. In the season for shedding, the fishermen call these beautiful swimmers "peelers." The meat that we buy fresh by the pound, however, is from the crabs with the hard shell. All crabmeat is perfect summer fare—very sapidus.

1. Pick over the crabmeat well, removing any cartilage. Mash it lightly, add the lemon juice, and mix.
2. Melt 2 tablespoons of butter in a heavy saucepan. Add the flour and blend until smooth. Add the milk slowly, beating with a whisk. Cook over medium-low heat until the sauce is smooth and has lost its raw flavor, 2 minutes. Blend in the egg yolks. Add the crabmeat, capers, salt, white pepper, and cayenne. (Seafood is especially compatible with cayenne as well as capers.)
3. Refrigerate the crabmeat mixture to allow it to firm up, at least 1 hour.
4. Prepare the coating: Make the breadcrumbs in a food processor (quicker and easier than a blender), using homemade-type white bread, and set aside in a bowl. Put the flour in a bowl, and beat together the egg and milk in another bowl.
5. Form the crabmeat mixture into 8 patties. Dip each patty in flour, then in the egg and milk mixture, and then coat well with breadcrumbs. Refrigerate for 1 hour or so to allow the crab cakes to set.
6. Heat the butter and oil in a heavy skillet and sauté the crab cakes until they are golden brown on both sides, 5 to 6 minutes. Serve with lemon wedges and homemade mayonnaise.

GRILLED BUTTERED TOAST

1. Preheat oven to 450°F. 2. Spread pieces of homemade-style white bread with butter on both sides. Put on a pastry sheet and place in the oven to grill. This will take from 8 to 10 minutes.

OYSTER PAN ROAST

[SERVES 4 TO 6]

For the true Chesapeake oyster lover, this is the dish.

> Shallot and White Wine Sauce (recipe follows) or lemon wedges
> 4 – 6 slices piping-hot Grilled Buttered Toast (see sidebar)
> 8 tablespoons (1 stick) unsalted butter
> 1 pint shucked fresh oysters, well drained
> Salt and freshly ground black pepper to taste
> Juice of 1 lemon
> Tabasco sauce to taste (optional)
> Several sprigs watercress, or chopped parsley, for garnish

1. Prepare the Shallot and White Wine Sauce, if using, and set aside.
2. Grill the toast.
3. In the meantime, melt the butter in a large heavy skillet. Place the oysters in the butter and cook over low heat just until the oysters have plumped and begun to curl. Quickly sprinkle with salt and pepper and the lemon juice.
4. Immediately place the hot oysters on the hot grilled toast. Sprinkle with the Tabasco, if desired. Garnish with watercress or chopped parsley, and serve with Shallot and White Wine Sauce or lemon wedges. Don't forget the chilled dry white wine or cold, cold beer.

SHALLOT AND WHITE WINE SAUCE

[MAKES ABOUT 1 CUP]

> 4 tablespoons (¹/₂ stick) unsalted butter, or more as needed
> ¹/₄ cup water
> ¹/₃ cup chopped shallots (do not substitute onions)
> ¹/₄ cup chopped red or green bell pepper (red is best)
> ¹/₂ cup dry white wine
> Salt and freshly ground black pepper to taste

1. In a heavy stainless-steel or enamel skillet, melt the butter in the water. Add the shallots and chopped bell pepper. Simmer until the water has boiled away, 2 minutes.
2. Add the wine and simmer until the mixture has lost its raw flavor, about 5 minutes. Add more butter if needed for the sauce to be smooth and creamy. Add salt and pepper to taste. Set aside.
3. Bring again to a simmer before pouring over the oysters on grilled toast.

THE GARDENER'S PRIDE

In planning which vegetables to have with certain menus, the season is our best guideline. The early Southern spring and sun-laden summers bring us green peas, asparagus, tender green beans, new potatoes, and corn, all of which are especially delicious with our lighter meals of fish, seafood, veal, and lamb. In the winter, the vibrant vegetables, such as acorn squash, cauliflower, cabbage, broccoli, and dried beans, are more compatible with the heartier meats, such as fresh pork, beef, and game; and there are almost no vegetables in the South that are incompatible with ham and chicken.

A steadfast rule that weathers all fads and fashions is that the vegetables must taste of what they are. It would be a shame to take great pains to grow fresh vegetables in the garden or to shop tirelessly for them in the market and then disguise their exquisite natural flavors by overcooking or overseasoning.

Freshness is at the heart of all fine vegetable cookery, and that freshness must be guarded jealously.

ASPARAGUS & TARRAGON SOUFFLÉ

[SERVES 4]

Wait to make this soufflé when the fresh tarragon is in, as it complements the asparagus and the cheese so knowingly.

1	pound fresh asparagus
3	tablespoons butter
3	tablespoons all-purpose flour
1	cup milk
1/4	cup freshly grated Parmesan or Swiss cheese
3	egg yolks
1	tablespoon chopped fresh tarragon
	Salt to taste
	Cayenne pepper to taste
4	egg whites

1. Preheat the oven to 375°F.
2. Break or cut off and discard the tough stem ends of the asparagus. Peel the stems with a thin sharp knife or vegetable peeler and cut the asparagus into 2-inch pieces. Drop into a pot of boiling salted water and cook only 2 to 3 minutes. The asparagus must remain crisp. Drain well.
3. Melt the butter in a heavy saucepan (enameled iron is good) or a double boiler. Add the flour and stir with a whisk until smooth. Add the milk slowly, whisking constantly; cook over medium-low heat until the sauce has thickened, 2 minutes. Add the cheese and blend. Stir in the egg yolks, tarragon, salt, and cayenne. Keep warm.
4. Put the asparagus in a buttered 4-cup shallow baking dish (see below).
5. Beat the egg whites with a pinch of salt until they are stiff but not dry and grainy. Fold a bit of the egg whites into the yolk and cheese mixture to lighten it, then add the mixture to the remaining egg whites, folding it in gently with a rubber spatula. Leave a few specks of egg white showing for greater volume. Spoon the mixture over the asparagus.
6. Place the dish on the middle or lower shelf of the oven and bake until the soufflé is well puffed and golden brown, 25 to 30 minutes. It should feel fairly firm to the touch. Serve immediately, remembering to scoop up the asparagus from the bottom.

• An oval baking dish is best for this soufflé, as it allows for a more even distribution of asparagus.

CLASSIC ASPARAGUS

ASPARAGUS POLONAISE: To 8 tablespoons melted butter in a small skillet, add 2 or 3 tablespoons breadcrumbs. Brown slightly and sprinkle over hot cooked asparagus.

FLEMISH ASPARAGUS: Mash the yolks of 2 or 3 hard-cooked eggs. Add 8 to 12 tablespoons melted butter to the yolks, making a sauce. Salt to taste. Serve in a sauceboat or over hot cooked asparagus. Sprinkle the asparagus with the chopped or sieved egg whites.

ASPARAGUS TARRAGON: Put freshly cooked and drained warm asparagus on lettuce. Cover with vinaigrette made with tarragon vinegar. Garnish with fresh tarragon if available.

ASPARAGUS MOUSSELINE: Blend 1/2 cup whipped cream into 1 1/2 cups hollandaise. Pour over hot cooked asparagus or serve in a sauceboat.

TO PREPARE ARTICHOKE BOTTOMS

Break off the artichoke stems. Tear off all the tough outer leaves, pulling each backward, then down toward the base. Using a small, well-sharpened stainless-steel (not carbon steel) knife, neatly pare the bottom where the stem has been torn off.

The pared surface of an artichoke darkens rapidly in contact with the air, so it is best to rub it with the cut surface of half a lemon several times during the process.

Plunge the pared artichokes into a stainless-steel or enamel saucepan of boiling water (to each quart add the juice of half a lemon and a pinch each of thyme and salt). Cook at a simmer until the flesh no longer resists a sharp knife or the tines of a cooking fork, 10 to 30 minutes, depending on the quality and age of the artichokes. They should remain firm. Cool them in the liquid and keep them well submerged, the receptacle covered and refrigerated, until ready to use. Before serving the artichokes, carefully remove them, using a teaspoon or small ice tongs to gently pry them loose. Wipe the artichoke bottoms with a towel.

ARTICHOKES BARIGOULE

[SERVES 4]

Barigoule is the old Provençal word for thyme. This recipe came from Mapie Lautrec, an in-law of the famous artist Toulouse-Lautrec, who, by the way, was a very good cook himself. Of all the stuffed artichokes I have met, this is the masterpiece. If you don't believe me, try it for lunch soon.

4	artichokes
	Salt and freshly ground black pepper to taste
2	shallots, chopped
1/4	cup chopped fresh parsley
1	teaspoon thyme (dried or fresh)
4	slices smoked bacon, diced
6	tablespoons good-quality olive oil, or more as needed
6	tablespoons white wine, or more as needed
1	clove garlic

1. Bring a large pot of salted water to a rolling boil.
2. Break off and discard the stem and cut off the top third of the artichokes. With scissors, trim off the thorny tips of the remaining leaves. Drop the artichokes into the water, season with salt and pepper, and cook at a low simmer until barely tender, 20 to 30 minutes. Turn the artichokes upside down in a colander to drain and discard the cooking water.
3. Remove the artichokes (see sidebar) and place the them back in the pot.
4. Combine the shallots, parsley, thyme, and bacon in a small bowl. Divide this mixture among the artichokes, placing a spoonful in the cavity of each one. Pour 1 tablespoon olive oil and 1 tablespoon wine into the cavity of each artichoke, and add the remaining 2 tablespoons each of oil and wine to the pot, around the artichokes. Place the garlic clove in the pot.
5. Cover the pot and cook over low heat for 35 to 40 minutes, adding more oil and wine to the pot if the mixture becomes dry—you want to have some sauce.
6. Spoon the sauce over the artichokes and serve.

VARIATIONS
- Use 1 tablespoon slivered baked ham instead of the bacon.
- Place 1 slice of peeled tomato in the cavity of each artichoke with the bacon or ham mixture.

CORN PUDDINGS

Corn puddings whey, or curdle, from prolonged or intense heat. They should be cooked in shallow baking dishes (the shallow 1½-quart heatproof glass ones are excellent). The typical American casseroles or soufflé dishes are too deep for corn pudding. By the time the heat has penetrated to the center of the pudding, the custard has curdled. A great deal of flour was used in the older recipes to overcome this. Few cooks seemed to blame the depth of the dish.

Tender corn puddings are made with little, if any, flour. The eggs and the starch from the corn are sufficient thickening agents.

EARLY SUMMER FRESH CORN PUDDING

[SERVES 6]

For those who like more corn than custard in their pudding, use 3 cups of corn, which should be about 9 ears.

6	ears tender fresh corn
3	eggs, beaten
1	cup heavy or whipping cream
⅓	cup milk
1	teaspoon salt
1	tablespoon sugar

1. Preheat the oven to 350°F.
2. Cut the corn from the cob and scrape the cobs well to extract the milk. You should have 2 cups of corn.
3. In a large bowl, mix the eggs, cream, and milk. Add the salt, sugar, and corn.
4. Pour the mixture into a buttered shallow casserole or heatproof glass dish. Place in a shallow pan of warm water and bake until a knife inserted in the center comes out clean, about 1 hour.

VARIATION

*   Corn and Red Bell Pepper Pudding: Add ¼ to ⅓ cup finely chopped red bell pepper with the corn, or use the sweet red pimiento pepper that ripens in the fall.

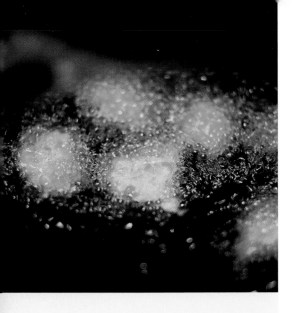

REMOULADE ROUGE OF NEW ORLEANS

[SERVES 4]

This is the red remoulade, spicy, hot, and delicious, that is served in New Orleans over chilled crawfish or shrimp as an appetizer or first course, or on lettuce as a salad with hot crunchy sourdough bread.

2   cups homemade mayonnaise
    (see page 60)

1½ teaspoons Creole or Dijon mustard

1½ tablespoons capers, drained

2   tablespoons of very finely
    chopped fresh parsley

2   tablespoons of very finely
    chopped fresh tarragon

2   teaspoons Hungarian paprika

1   teaspoon cayenne pepper

    Juice of ½ lemon, or to taste

1   clove garlic

1   pound cooked small shrimp
    or cooked crawfish

1. Combine all the ingredients except the shrimp or crawfish in a bowl and mix well. Cover tightly and refrigerate for 1 to 3 hours. Discard the garlic.......
2. Serve over crawfish or small shrimp with hot toasted crackers or French bread.

OLD STONE INN CORN FRITTERS

[SERVES 4 TO 6]

This makes a round ball-type fritter—delicious but sturdy.

6   ears tender fresh corn

3   eggs, separated

$^7/_8$ cup sifted all-purpose flour

1   teaspoon salt

1   teaspoon sugar

    Cayenne pepper to taste

2   teaspoons baking powder

    Oil for deep-frying

1. Cut the corn from the cobs and scrape the cobs well to extract the milk. You should have 1½ to 2 cups of corn. Mash ¼ cup of the corn pulp with a potato masher or in a blender or food processor. (This helps to distribute the corn flavor and extract some starch.) Return it to the rest of the corn.

2. Mix the egg yolks with the corn. Sift together the flour, salt, sugar, cayenne, and baking powder. Add to the corn and mix well.

3. Beat the egg whites until stiff but not dry and grainy, and fold them into the corn mixture.

4. Heat the oil in a deep-fat fryer to about 375°F. Drop the batter by tablespoonfuls into the fat and cook the fritters until browned on one side, about 2 minutes. Turn, and when both sides are golden brown remove with a slotted spoon and drain on paper towels. Serve at once with fried chicken or broiled country ham.

OLD-FASHIONED GREENS

[SERVES 6]

When you are offered old-fashioned greens cooked with slab bacon or ham hock, and served with corn muffins, you know you are south of the Mason-Dixon line. The greens all have different flavors, so the choice is up to the cook. Always pass the vinegar to be sprinkled on the greens.

2	pounds greens, such as turnip greens, mustard greens, collard greens, or kale, or mixed as desired
$1/2$	pound slab smoked bacon, or 1-pound piece smoked ham hock
3	quarts water
$1/2$	small pod dried or fresh chile pepper, or to taste, slivered
	Salt to taste

1. Select fresh tender greens with no yellow leaves. Remove and discard the stems. Set aside.

2. Add the bacon or ham hock to 3 quarts of water in a large stainless-steel or enamel pot and allow to boil, uncovered, for 30 to 40 minutes. The water should be reduced by half.

3. In the meantime, wash the greens in at least 3 changes of water, swishing them about to rid them of sand. Lift the greens out of the water each time. Drain.

4. Add the greens to the pot. Add the chile pepper and allow the greens to simmer long and slowly until they are really tender, 1 hour. The greens should be simmered no more than $1/2$ inch below the stock line. Strain off any extra stock and add it to the pot only if needed as the greens cook. Taste for salt when the greens are almost done; as the bacon and ham hock are salty, it may be unnecessary to add any. Discard the bacon or ham hock, drain the greens, if necessary, and serve.

THE SECRET OF GREAT GREENS

A delicious pot of greens is never made with bacon fat or "drippings." The best flavor comes from the un-cooked smoked bacon or ham hock, never salt pork. It is not worth the trouble to clean the greens if bacon drippings are to be used. All you are getting is grease.

GREEN PEAS

Green Peas are the most beloved and delicate of our early summer vegetables. They came originally from the lands around the Nile. Dried peas have been found in ancient Egyptian tombs, and they were so generally known in England during the Middle Ages that the word "porridge" became synonymous with them. Remember the nursery rhyme "Peas porridge hot, Peas porridge cold"? It sings of green peas—not at all of a gummy, hot cereal as some have thought.

VIDALIA ONION PIE
[SERVES 6]

3	tablespoons butter
5	medium Vidalia onions, thinly sliced
1	partially baked 9-inch Standard Pastry Crust (see page 223)
1	cup grated aged Swiss cheese
2	whole eggs
2	egg yolks
1	cup milk
$^1/_2$	cup heavy or whipping cream
1	teaspoon salt
	Cayenne pepper to taste

1. Preheat the oven to 350°F.
2. Melt the butter in a heavy saucepan. Add the onions and cook over medium-low heat until they are limp but not the least bit brown.
3. Drain the onions and arrange them in the pastry shell. Cover the onions with the grated cheese.
4. Beat the eggs, egg yolks, milk, and cream together. Season with salt and cayenne pepper, and pour over the cheese.
5. Place the pie pan on the lower shelf of the oven and bake until the pie has puffed in the middle and is golden brown all over, 35 to 40 minutes.

THE MIGHTY POTATO &
THE MAGNIFICENT GRAINS

In spite of our casual acceptance of the white potato, this life-sustaining root vegetable is one of our favorites. Originally kept in the flower garden as a novelty, it was thought to be poisonous long before it was accepted and admired as food. Are there any among us who aren't fond of potatoes, mashed to perfection and seasoned well with "oodles" of butter? Not one.

The sweet potato is as native to the Southern states as corn is. It was known in colonial days as the potato of Virginia, and although it isn't as useful as the white potato, it takes its natural place with ham and the Thanksgiving turkey.

One of our favorite of the grains is hominy, or grits, made from the South's native corn. We love grits cooked almost any way. When you are served grits hot for breakfast along with your eggs and bacon or sausage—without even ordering them—then you know you are deep inside Dixie.

Rice, the most venerable of all the grains, has deep roots in the South. Texas and Louisiana produce the largest volume of rice today, and South Carolina was the first among the early colonies to grow the grain. It is well documented that in 1787 Thomas Jefferson, ever the agronomist, smuggled a small bag of rice out of Italy when he was on a diplomatic mission there. It was this rice that provided the seed to revive the stricken Carolina rice industry after the Revolutionary War.

SPRING MEADOW POTATOES

[SERVES 6]

There is a fresh and incomparable flavor in new potatoes. I mean the ones that are fresh from the earth in which they grew—not those that have been dyed red to fool us! These potatoes, when cooked with ham and served with a green vegetable, a salad of cottage cheese on lettuce with a dollop of sour cream, and Hoe Cake, make a beautiful Southern meal.

2	pounds tiny new potatoes
	Water or Chicken, Veal, or White Soup Stock (see pages 38 and 39)
$^1/_4$	cup slivered baked smoked ham
3	tablespoons butter, at room temperature
	Salt, if needed
	Freshly ground white pepper to taste
3	tablespoons chopped fresh chives
3	tablespoons chopped fresh parsley

1. Select small, firm new potatoes. Cut out any blemishes and peel away a ribbon of skin around the center of each potato. (There is lots of good flavor in fresh new potato skins.)
2. Bring the water or stock to a boil and drop in the potatoes. There should be enough liquid to cover the potatoes by 3 inches. Add the ham and cook until the potatoes are tender, 30 minutes.
3. Drain the potatoes and toss them with the butter, and salt and white pepper to taste. Sprinkle with the chives and parsley, and serve.

VARIATION

• If you have some extra-good smoked bacon, it can be partially broiled and used instead of the ham. The bacon must not be crisp, as that changes the flavor of the entire dish.

CHIVES

Chives are a member of the onion family, and a soft-spoken one. They are most pleasant used in salads and sandwiches where just a hint of onion flavor is needed.

ALFRED LUNT'S POTATOES

[SERVES 6]

Leftover baked potatoes, if the skin is not broken, develop a "nutty" flavor. The actor Alfred Lunt, who gave some cooking lessons for the U.S.O. in Washington, D.C. during World War II, taught me this.

6   baked potatoes,
    chilled with their skin on

8   tablespoons (1 stick) butter

1   teaspoon salt, or to taste

2   tablespoons chopped fresh dill

1   tablespoon chopped fresh parsley

1. Preheat the oven to 400°F. 2. Slice the potatoes very thin and lay them in a buttered baking pan, each slice slightly overlapping the one next to it. Dot with the butter and sprinkle with salt. 3. Bake until golden brown and crunchy, 25 to 30 minutes. 4. Sprinkle with the chopped dill and parsley.

OLD-FASHIONED HOME-FRIED POTATOES

[SERVES 6]

Serve with steak, ground steak patties, or veal chops. Notable with scrambled eggs or as a filling for an omelet.

3   tablespoons fresh bacon fat

5   Idaho potatoes, thinly sliced

3   slices bacon, diced

1   sweet onion, thinly sliced
    Salt and freshly ground black pepper to taste
    Chopped fresh parsley, for garnish

1. Heat the bacon fat in a heavy iron skillet. Add the potatoes, bacon, and onion and cook, covered, over medium heat 10 to 15 minutes. Shake the pan while the potatoes are cooking so the bacon and onion will not burn (you can place the bacon and onion on top of the potatoes to prevent burning). Turn the potatoes from time to time with a spatula and try to keep the onion on top.

2. Remove the cover and continue cooking until the potatoes are golden brown and crunchy, 10 to 12 minutes. Sprinkle with salt, pepper, and parsley.

DEEP-FRIED SWEET POTATOES

[SERVES 6]

You will find that fried sweet potatoes or yams are more delicious if they have been boiled first—it brings out their flavor. In Florida they sprinkle them with sugar. Your sweet tooth, or lack of one, will guide you. I have a sweet tooth. Serve with broiled ham, warm baked ham, or broiled or fried chicken.

2   pounds sweet potatoes or yams
    Oil for deep-frying
    Salt or sugar (optional)

1. Drop the sweet potatoes in boiling salted water to cover by 3 or 4 inches. Remove them before they are thoroughly cooked, 20 to 25 minutes. Cool the potatoes, then peel and cut them into pieces about 2 inches long and $^1/_2$ inch thick.

2. Heat the oil in a deep-fat fryer to 375°F.

3. Plunge the potato sticks into the oil a few at a time and cook only until light brown. Remove, drain on paper towels, and sprinkle with salt or sugar. Keep warm while you fry the rest.

ALABAMA YAMS WITH ORANGES

[SERVES 6 TO 8]

This is the Deep South's way with yams or sweet potatoes. It seems to always show up with the Thanksgiving turkey, but it is just as compatible with a good ham or chicken. Do not peel either the potatoes or the orange. If you don't have a luscious rich sauce, you have been too cautious with the butter.

6	yams or sweet potatoes, fully cooked and cooled
3	navel oranges, thinly sliced
$^1/_2$ – $^3/_4$ cup (1 to 1$^1/_2$ sticks) butter	
$^3/_4$	cup sugar
1	cup fresh orange juice
2	tablespoons fresh lemon juice, or more to taste

1. Preheat the oven to 375°F.
2. Peel and slice the sweet potatoes very thin and place one layer in a shallow buttered baking dish. Top with a layer of orange slices. Dot generously with butter and sprinkle with sugar. Continue layering. You should have three layers, ending with a layer of potatoes, butter, and sugar.
3. Mix the orange juice with the lemon juice and pour it over the potatoes.
4. Bake until a pleasant syrup has formed and the top is tinged with brown, 1$^1/_2$ hours.

YAMS OR SWEET POTATOES WITH LEMON

Omit the sliced oranges and orange juice. Season the layers of potatoes with the grated peel of 1$^1/_2$ lemons, the sugar, and the juice of 2 lemons combined with $^1/_3$ cup water. Use the full $^3/_4$ cup of butter. A favorite that's nice with duck.

STEAMED WHITE RICE

[SERVES 4]

Measure 1 cup white long- or medium-grain rice, 2 cups water, and 1 teaspoon salt into a heavy saucepan. Place over high heat, and when the water boils vigorously, stir several times and cover with a tight-fitting lid. Turn the heat very low and cook 14 minutes.

Turn off the heat, fluff the grains with a fork, replace the cover, and allow the rice to steam. The water should be completely absorbed and the grains separate, flaky, and tender, but with some firmness, 4 to 5 minutes.

For extra-tender rice, start with $1/3$ cup more water and increase the cooking time by 4 to 5 minutes.

DEEP SOUTH RED BEANS & RICE

[SERVES 6 TO 8]

Many recipes for Red Beans and Rice call for dried kidney beans, but the dried dark-red round bean is the authentic bean.

1	pound dried red beans
3	quarts water, or more as needed
$1/4$	pound slice uncooked ham or $1/2$ small ham hock
1	medium onion
2	ribs celery, cut in half
2	bay leaves
2	sprigs fresh thyme or $1/2$ teaspoon dried
$1/4$	small fresh or dried red chile pepper to taste
2	cups freshly cooked white rice
	Salt and black pepper to taste
	Chopped fresh parsley, for garnish

1. Wash the beans thoroughly. Bring $1^1/2$ quarts of the water to a boil in a large pot, add the beans, and boil 5 minutes.

2. Remove the pot from the heat and allow the beans to soak 1 hour.

3. Drain the beans and set them aside.

4. Add $1^1/2$ quarts of fresh water to the pot. Add the ham or ham hock, onion, celery, bay leaves, thyme, and chile pepper. Bring to a boil and cook 20 minutes. (This seasons the stock.) Add the red beans and simmer until they are tender but not mushy, about 1 hour.

5. Discard the meat, onion, celery, and bay leaves. Add salt and pepper to taste. There should be a little sauce, but the beans must not be soupy. If there is too much sauce, reduce it quickly over high heat.

6. Serve the beans over the rice. Sprinkle with the parsley.

CORN

The basic elements of corn are the hull, the germ, and the endosperm. Corn is steamed first, to loosen the hull. Then the grains are split and the hull and the germ removed. What remains is the endosperm, the part that is made into grits and cornmeal. The endosperm is passed through heavy steel rollers that break it into granules. The largest of these granules become grits, the medium ones become cornmeal, and the finest are corn flour.

A CASSEROLE OF GRITS

[SERVES 6]

The cooking time depends upon the kind of grits used. The old-fashioned long-cooking grits have more flavor than precooked grits. Serve this dish with broiled ham or chicken, sautéed quail, or pheasant.

4	cups water
1	teaspoon salt
$^3/_4$	cup hominy grits
$5^1/_2$	tablespoons butter
3 – 4	eggs, beaten
	Salt to taste
	Cayenne pepper to taste

1. Bring the water and salt to a boil, add the grits, and simmer, stirring constantly, over medium heat until the grits taste done and are thick and perfectly smooth, about 20 minutes.
2. Preheat the oven to 350°F.
3. When the grits are done, add 4 tablespoons of the butter, the eggs, salt, and cayenne. Stir well. Pour the mixture into a buttered shallow casserole and dot with the remaining butter.
4. Bake until the grits are golden brown, 25 to 30 minutes.

•   When boiling grits, 5 parts water to 1 part grits is about perfect. Using 3 eggs makes a nice casserole, but 4 eggs makes it richer and gives it greater volume.

PASTA MACHINES

All the doughs included here are easy to roll in a pasta machine. If you are lucky enough to own one, follow the directions for uniformly cut noodles included with your machine. If you are using a pasta machine, dust the dough generously with flour as needed to prevent it from sticking. It will not toughen the noodles.

WATERCRESS NOODLES WITH WALNUTS

[SERVES 4]

Watercress noodles are a most elegant and appetizing shade of green and are far superior to spinach noodles. They are rich but do not have an assertive watercress flavor. Serve these beautiful noodles with walnuts as a light entrée or with a veal chop, broiled ham or chicken, sautéed rabbit, chicken, or sweetbreads. The veal chop is especially delicious.

1	teaspoon butter
$^1/_3$	cup walnut pieces
$^1/_2$	pound Watercress Noodles (see recipe below)
6	tablespoons walnut oil or unsalted butter, warmed
	Salt and freshly ground white pepper to taste
2	tablespoons chopped fresh parsley
	Lemon juice to taste

1. Bring a large kettle of salted water to a boil.
2. Meanwhile, melt the butter in a skillet over low heat. Add the walnuts and toss continuously until they are a bit crisper. Do not allow them to brown. Set aside.
3. Drop the noodles into the boiling water and cook until tender, 4 minutes. Drain thoroughly.
4. Toss the hot noodles into a large warm bowl. Add the warmed walnut oil or butter and stir well.

Add the walnuts, salt, white pepper, parsley, and lemon juice. Serve at once.

WATERCRESS NOODLES

[MAKES ABOUT 1 POUND]

$^1/_2$	pound watercress (2 large bunches)
2	cups all-purpose flour, sifted
2	eggs
1	egg yolk
2	teaspoons good-quality olive or vegetable oil
1	teaspoon salt

1. Remove the coarsest stems from the watercress, leaving the tender stems intact. Drop the watercress into lightly salted boiling water and boil until the stems are tender, 3 to 4 minutes. The watercress must retain its bright color. Drain at once.
2. Purée watercress in a processor or blender until mixture is perfectly fine and no stem pieces are showing.
3. Spread the watercress out on several thicknesses of paper towels. Cover with more paper towels

BALTIMORE.

and pat heavily so the towels will absorb the water. Repeat this process several times, until the watercress is like a dried green curd. You should have 3 to 4 tablespoons.

4. To prepare the noodles by hand: Sift the flour into a large wooden bowl or onto a clean flat surface. Make a well in the center of the flour. In a bowl, combine the eggs, yolk, oil, salt, and watercress curd. Blend thoroughly, and pour into the center of the flour. With a fork, blend the flour little by little into the watercress mixture, using more flour as needed. Knead for about 4 minutes. The dough should be soft, pliable, and not the least bit sticky. Cover the dough and allow it to rest 1 hour in the refrigerator before rolling.

5. To prepare the noodles in a processor: Combine the eggs, yolk, oil, salt, and watercress curd in a processor. Blend. Add the flour to the watercress mixture quickly while the processor is running. Process just a few seconds. Toss the dough onto a lightly floured surface and knead until it is soft, pliable, and not sticky, adding a little sifted flour as needed, 4 minutes. Cover the dough and allow it to rest 1 hour in the refrigerator before rolling.

6. Roll the dough out by hand until it is $1/16$ to $1/8$ inch thick, and cut into noodles; or roll and cut on a pasta machine, following the manufacturer's directions.

Watercress noodle dough will freeze well either in a flat cake, to thaw and roll out later, or cut into noodles.

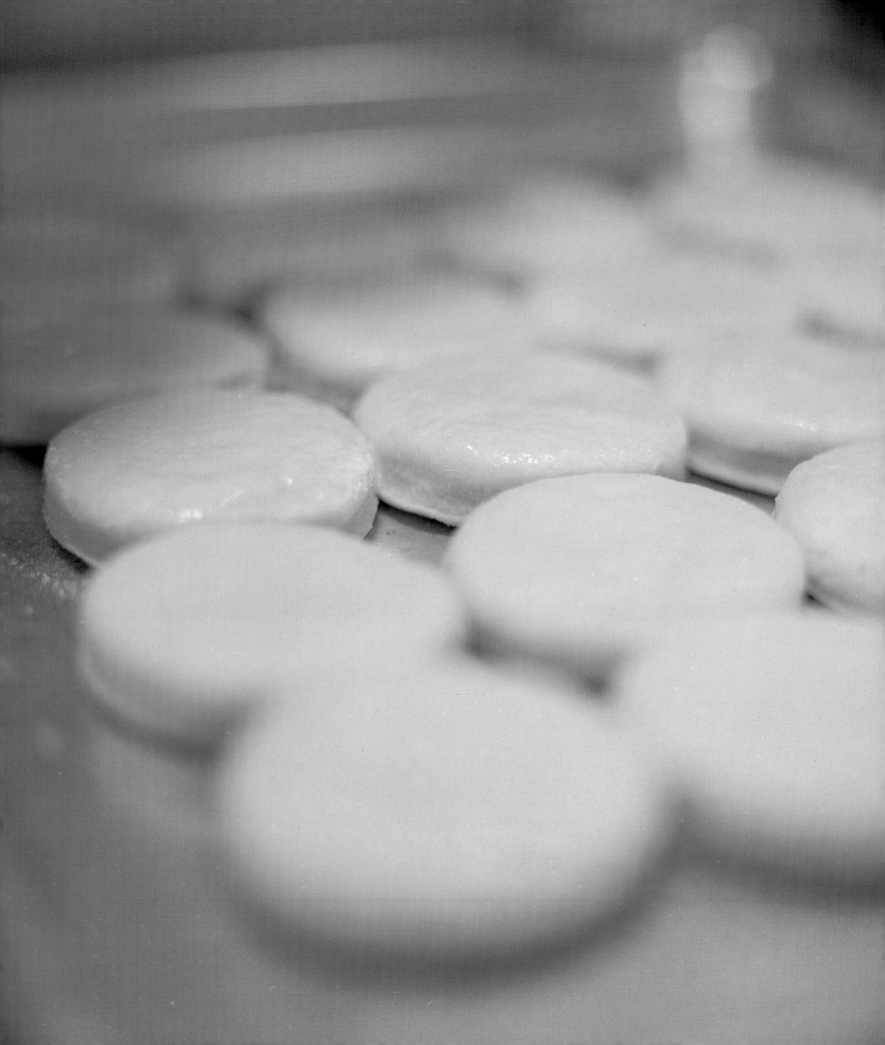

BREAD WINNERS

Our homemade Southern breads and rolls, we are told, have a character all their own. Our cornbreads and muffins, of course, are native to our cuisine and they do have, just as they should, a great affinity for many of our favorite Southern dishes. Heavy, coarse cornmeals are praised by some, but elegant, feathery-light cornbreads are made with finely ground white (not yellow) cornmeal, and never corn flour.

Our yeast rolls and biscuits have, I believe, remained somewhat unique. In fact, hot homemade breads of all kinds have been a cornerstone of our menus. For breakfast or lunch, for tea in the afternoon, or for dinner, we have a repertoire of delicious breads to choose from.

For those who like to bake, and Southern cooks are bakers, it is a rich heritage, and one that we like to share with others.

ELIZABETH CHOWNING'S DIVINE BREAD

[MAKES 2 LOAVES]

This is one of the most divine of Southern breads—so much so that it named itself. It ages better than most breads, it freezes well, and it has an exquisite flavor. The variations are endless; the glazed pear, apricot, or yellow plum bread makes you want to live and live—bake and bake.

2	packages dry yeast
$1^{1}/_{2}$	cups lukewarm water
$^{1}/_{2}$	cup sugar
1	tablespoon salt
4	tablespoons ($^{1}/_{2}$ stick) unsalted butter, melted
4	large eggs
7	cups sifted all-purpose flour
1	egg yolk, beaten
2	tablespoons heavy or whipping cream
	Poppy seeds, for garnish

1. Dissolve the yeast in the water in a large bowl, or in the bowl of an electric mixer or food processor.
2. Add the sugar, salt, butter, and eggs and mix thoroughly. Add about $6^{1}/_{2}$ cups flour, 1 cup at a time, mixing well.
3. Turn the dough out onto a lightly floured surface and knead it for 3 minutes. Add just enough of the remaining flour to keep it from being sticky. (Too much flour makes this bread heavy.)
4. Put the dough in a large greased bowl and turn it to coat the surface. Cover the bowl with plastic wrap and leave it in a warm place until the dough has doubled in bulk, 1 to $1^{1}/_{4}$ hours. (If after the rising the dough still seems too sticky to work with, chill it thoroughly. Cold dough is always easier to manage.)
5. Punch the dough down, and roll it out on a lightly floured surface to rid it of air bubbles. Make 2 free-form loaves.
6. Place the loaves on a lightly greased or nonstick baking sheet. Cover with plastic wrap and leave in a warm spot until the dough has doubled in bulk again, about $1^{1}/_{4}$ hours. The dough should feel light and springy.
7. Preheat the oven to 350°F.
8. Mix the egg yolk thoroughly with the cream and brush the tops of the loaves with the glaze. Sprinkle with poppy seeds.
9. Place the baking sheet on the middle shelf of the oven and bake until the bread is golden brown and sounds hollow when rapped with your knuckle, 45 to 50 minutes.
10. Turn the loaves out onto a rack, turning them several times during the cooling process.

VARIATIONS

DIVINE BRAIDS: Prepare the dough through step 5, dividing it in half. Cut each half into 3 even strips. Braid the strips into two loaves, pinching the ends under. Proceed with step 6.

DIVINE MINK STOLES: Make up the dough through step 4. Punch the dough down and roll it out $^{1}/_{2}$ inch thick and 6 inches wide on a lightly floured surface. Cut into strips 1 inch wide. Fold each strip in the shape of a mink stole crossed over your shoulders. Place the stoles about 3 inches apart on a lightly greased or nonstick baking sheet. Cover loosely with plastic wrap and allow the rolls to rise until light and springy, 45 minutes to 1 hour. Brush them with the mixture of egg yolk and cream, and sprinkle them with poppy seeds. Bake on the middle shelf of a preheated 375°F oven until golden brown, 20 to 25 minutes. Serve warm or cold.

SOUTHERN HERITAGE
POTATO ROLLS

[MAKES ABOUT 45 ROLLS]

Prepare the dough as directed, forming it into small rounds with a floured biscuit cutter in step 5. (The rolls may be brushed generously with butter, covered with plastic wrap, and refrigerated for 1 day or overnight. Remove from the refrigerator and allow to rise until doubled in bulk, about 3 hours.) Bake them in a preheated 375°F oven for 10 to 12 minutes.

SOUTHERN HERITAGE POTATO BREAD

[MAKES 2 LOAVES]

This rich potato bread is exquisitely moist and delicious. It is also redolent of our early breads, as the sponge is made up and allowed to rise and ferment to a small degree the night before baking.

1	package dry yeast
$1/4$	cup lukewarm water
1	large mealy potato (about 12 ounces)
$2/3$	cup sugar
4	eggs, beaten
1	cup (2 sticks) unsalted butter, at room temperature
2	teaspoons salt
$6^{1}/_{2}$ – 7	cups sifted all-purpose flour
$1^{1}/_{2}$	teaspoons butter, melted

1. Dissolve the yeast in the water.
2. Peel and coarsely chop the potato. Place it in a small saucepan, cover with water, and cook over medium heat until soft, 20 to 25 minutes. Drain the potato, but reserve $3/4$ cup of the cooking water and keep it warm. Sieve or rice the warm potato into a large mixing bowl and add the reserved potato water, the dissolved yeast, and the sugar. Mix well. Cover with foil and leave to rise overnight at room temperature.
3. The next morning, add the eggs, butter, and salt. (This is done easily in a heavy-duty electric mixer.) Blend thoroughly. Add the flour, 2 cups at a time, beating hard. When 6 cups of flour have been added, turn the dough onto a lightly floured surface. Knead the dough, while adding extra flour, until it is velvety and soft but not sticky, 4 minutes.
4. Place the dough in a large greased bowl and turn it to coat the surface. Cover the bowl with plastic wrap and leave it in a warm, draft-free spot until the dough has doubled in bulk, about $1^{1}/_{2}$ hours.
5. Punch the dough down, cut it in half, and roll each half out $1/2$ inch thick on a lightly floured surface to rid it of air bubbles. Roll up each half as you would a jelly roll and place the loaves, tucking the ends under, in 2 greased standard $9^{1}/_{2}$ x $4^{1}/_{2}$ x 3-inch) loaf pans. Brush the tops with melted butter. Cover the pans with plastic wrap and allow the dough to double in bulk again, 2 hours or more. (Do not place this dough in an overly warm place. If the large amount of butter melts before baking, the texture will be grainy.)
6. Preheat the oven to 375°F.
7. Bake the bread on the middle shelf of the oven until it is golden brown and sounds hollow when rapped with your knuckle, about 45 minutes. Watch it carefully—don't overbake.
8. Turn the loaves out onto a rack to cool, turning them several times during the cooling process.

TESTING FOR DONENESS

Breads can be tested for doneness by inserting a cake tester, skewer, or thin knife in the center of the loaf. If it comes out clean, with no crumbs attached, the bread is done.

You can also test a bread by rapping it with your knuckle. If the bread sounds hollow, it is most likely done.

Tea breads can be tested by pressing down lightly on the center with your fingers. If the bread springs back quickly, it is done.

MONTICELLO ROLLS

[MAKES 36 ROLLS]

This is a lovely, velvety dough, and it is typical of the fine hot breads that are made in the South. Yeast doughs rich in eggs and butter are not kneaded as heavily as lean doughs (flour, yeast, shortening, and water), and they keep better before baking.

1	package dry yeast
1/4	cup lukewarm water
1	large mealy potato
4	tablespoons (1/2 stick) butter, cut into pieces
2	tablespoons sugar
2	eggs
1 1/2	teaspoons salt
3 1/2	cups all-purpose flour, sifted
6	tablespoons (3/4 stick) butter, melted

1. Dissolve the yeast in the water.

2. Peel and coarsely chop the potato. Place it in a small saucepan, cover with water, and cook over medium heat until soft, 20 to 25 minutes. Drain the potato but reserve the cooking water. Keep it warm.

3. While it is still hot, sieve or rice the potato into a large bowl (not a food processor—it will turn the potato gummy). Add butter and 1/4 cup of the warm potato water. Mix by hand or with an electric mixer until the butter has melted.

4. Add the sugar and eggs and mix well. Add the dissolved yeast and the salt. Beat in 3 cups of the flour, 1 cup at a time, until you have a malleable dough.

5. Lift the dough onto a lightly floured surface. Knead it lightly, adding enough extra flour to keep the dough from being overly sticky, about 2 minutes. This is a soft dough, and too much flour will make the rolls dry instead of light and moist.

6. Put the dough in a greased bowl and turn it to coat the surface. Cover the bowl with plastic wrap and leave it in a warm spot until the dough has doubled in bulk, about 1 hour. (After the dough has doubled, it can be punched down, covered, and refrigerated until well chilled, or overnight if desired, before forming it into rolls.)

7. Place the dough on a lightly floured surface. Knead it gently for 1 minute. Roll out the dough 1/4 inch thick. Cut it into circles with a 2 1/2-inch biscuit cutter.

8. Brush the tops with some of the melted butter. With the dull edge of a knife, press a crease just off-center in each round. Fold the dough over so that the larger part overlaps the smaller.

9. Place the folded rolls, barely touching each other, on a nonstick or lightly greased baking sheet, and put it in a warm spot free of drafts. Cover with plastic wrap and allow the dough to double in

bulk again, about 45 minutes. It should spring back at once when lightly touched.

10. Preheat the oven to 375°F.

11. Place the baking sheet on the middle shelf of the oven and bake until the rolls are golden brown, and a skewer inserted in the center of a roll comes out clean, 15 to 20 minutes. Brush immediately with more melted butter. Serve piping hot.

If the rolls do not touch, they are likely to spring open when rising or baking.

SOUTHERN BUTTERMILK BISCUITS

[MAKES 25 TO 30 BISCUITS]

This is the true Southern biscuit—made with buttermilk, rolled not too thick, and baked until golden brown. We like them with sausage and grits for a leisurely breakfast or with fried chicken anytime. They are a perennial favorite for cocktail parties and receptions when cut small and served piping hot, filled with sliced baked country ham. Now, can you think of anything better? I don't believe you can.

2	cups all-purpose flour, plus more as needed
$\frac{1}{4}$	teaspoon baking soda
1	tablespoon baking powder
1	teaspoon salt
6	tablespoons lard or solid vegetable shortening
$\frac{3}{4}$	cup buttermilk

1. Sift the dry ingredients into a roomy bowl. Cut in the shortening with a pastry blender or fork until the mixture has the texture of coarse meal. Add the buttermilk and mix with your hand, lightly but thoroughly. Add a little more flour if the dough is too sticky. Knead for 1 minute. Wrap in waxed paper or foil and refrigerate until well chilled, at least 20 minutes.

2. Preheat the oven to 450°F.

3. Roll the dough out $\frac{1}{2}$ inch thick on a lightly floured surface or pastry cloth. (Always roll from the center out for tender, crisp biscuits.) Cut the dough into the desired size biscuits.

4. Place the biscuits on a dark baking sheet and bake until golden brown, 10 to 12 minutes.

- If some dough is left over, it is wiser to bake the biscuits and freeze them, as the buttermilk dough will not keep for more than 10 to 12 hours.

VARIATIONS

- CHEESE BISCUITS: Work $\frac{1}{4}$ to $\frac{1}{2}$ cup freshly grated sharp natural Cheddar or Parmesan cheese into the dough before rolling it out $\frac{3}{8}$ inch thick. Cut into small biscuits and bake in a preheated 375° to 400°F oven. Serve with salad for luncheons, or for cocktails.

- ROSEMARY BISCUITS: A favorite. Work $\frac{1}{2}$ to 1 teaspoon crushed dried rosemary into the dough before rolling it out $\frac{1}{2}$ inch thick. Cut into 2- to $2\frac{1}{2}$-inch biscuits. Serve with sausage, pork, or lamb. Especially delicious as small biscuits served with smoked country sausage for a wintertime hors d'oeuvre or a Sunday brunch.

MAKING BISCUITS

Lard makes a crisper biscuit than vegetable shortening. To make biscuits with a smooth top, the dough must be covered and thoroughly chilled, then kneaded lightly but well.

Overkneading biscuit dough brings out the gluten and toughens the biscuits. Too much flour on the pastry board will also toughen the biscuits. A pastry cloth helps prevent the need for extra flour.

Biscuits must be baked in a very hot oven or they will toughen.

CORNMEAL SPOONBREAD SOUFFLE

[SERVES 6 TO 8]

This Southern heritage spoonbread is so light and delectable that it had to be called a soufflé. It is delicious with all kinds of chicken and ham dishes, and especially with veal and rabbit stews.

2	cups milk
5	tablespoons fine white cornmeal
2	tablespoons butter
1	teaspoon salt
3	eggs, separated
1 $^1/_2$	teaspoons baking powder

1. Preheat the oven to 350°F.
2. Scald the milk in a heavy saucepan, but do not allow it to boil. Add the cornmeal and cook over medium heat, whisking constantly, until the mixture is like thick mush, about 5 minutes. Add the butter and salt. When the butter has melted, add the egg yolks and baking powder.
3. Beat the egg whites until they are stiff but not dry and grainy. Fold them into the cornmeal mixture.
4. Pour the batter into a buttered 1-quart soufflé dish or a 1$^1/_2$-quart shallow baking dish. Bake until lightly browned. Depending on the type of dish used, this will take 30 to 40 minutes. Serve at once.

MAKING A SOUFFLE COLLAR

1. Cut a sheet of foil that will encircle the soufflé dish with the ends over-lapping about one inch, and that will extend from the bottom of the dish to three inches above the top when folded in half lengthwise. 2. Fold the foil strip in half lengthwise, and brush the top four inches of the foil on one side with soft butter. 3. Wrap the collar, with the buttered foil facing in, around the outside of the soufflé dish. Fasten the ends tightly with freezer tape or paper clips, or tie a string around the dish to hold the collar on. The foil must fit snugly so the soufflé will extend securely above the top of the dish.

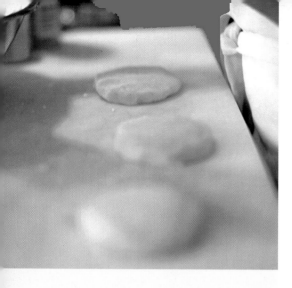

HOE CAKES

[MAKES 6 TO 8 CAKES]

We do not know the lineage of the name "hoe cake." It was a favorite bread of country people in the South, but it was not baked on a hoe. That would have been impossible. If you enjoy cornmeal and you like the texture of a hot, crisp bread, you will love hoe cakes when they are served with the right menu. These are delicious with an all-vegetable meal, or with hearty bean and vegetable soups. Marvelous with a wilted lettuce or spinach salad.

1   cup fine white cornmeal

1   teaspoon salt

1   tablespoon lard or solid vegetable shortening

$3/4$ cup boiling water, or as needed

    Lard or solid vegetable shortening (see step 3)

1.   Combine the cornmeal, salt, and lard or shortening. Mix well.

2.   Slowly add water that is boiling hard to the meal, mixing thoroughly and quickly. When the mixture is soft but not too wet, form it into thin $2^{1}/_{2}$-inch cakes.

3.   Melt enough lard or shortening on a heavy black iron griddle to form a thick coating. When the griddle is very hot, but not smoking, add the hoe cakes, a few at a time, and fry until one side is golden brown, 2 to 3 minutes. Turn and brown the second side. Drain on paper towels and serve at once.

•   If the imprint of your fingers will not stay on the hoe cakes when they are formed, you have used too much water.

HUSH PUPPIES

[SERVES 4]

2   cups white cornmeal

1   teaspoon salt

2   tablespoons chopped scallions (green onions)

1   cup milk, or more as needed

2   eggs

$1/4$ cup lard or vegetable shortening, melted

    Oil, for deep frying

1. Combine the cornmeal, salt, and scallions in a medium bowl. Mix well, then add the milk, eggs, and melted shortening, and mix again. The mixture must not be crumbly. Add more milk if necessary. 2. Heat the oil in a deep-fat fryer to 375°F. 3. Form the batter into $1^{1}/_{2}$-inch balls and fry them a few at a time until they are light golden brown, 2 to 3 minutes. Drain on paper towels and serve at once.

Lard makes a crispier hush puppy than does vegetable shortening.

ST. PETERSBURG ORANGE & APRICOT BREAD

[MAKES 2 SMALL LOAVES]

A fine cook from St. Petersburg gave me this bread years ago and it has been a favorite ever since. Wonderful for tea, breakfast, lunch, or just when you want to taste something delicious.

USING DRIED APRICOTS

Drain the apricots well or there will be too much moisture and the bread will be heavy. The oven temperature must be kept low, as this loaf burns easily. The whole apricots will show up in an attractive pattern when the bread is sliced.

1	package (7 ounces) dried apricots
1	egg
1	cup sugar
2	tablespoons butter, melted and cooled
2	cups all-purpose flour
3/4	teaspoon salt
3/4	cup fresh orange juice
1	teaspoon grated orange peel
1	tablespoon baking powder

1. Soak the apricots in warm water to cover for 30 minutes.
2. Preheat the oven to 325°F.
3. Drain the apricots thoroughly, setting aside a few of them aside to be added to the batter whole. Mash the remaining apricots with a fork. Do not purée.
4. Combine the egg and sugar in a large bowl and beat with an electric mixer until the mixture drops from the spoon in ribbons. Beat in the melted butter.
5. Sift the flour with the salt. Add it to the flour mixture alternately with the orange juice and grated peel. Add the baking powder and mix it in quickly. Add the mashed apricots and mix thoroughly. Fold in the whole pieces of apricot by hand.
6. Spoon the batter into 2 small (7 x 4 x 2-inch) foil-lined pans. Set the pans on the middle shelf of the oven and bake until the batter springs back at once when lightly touched, about 1 hour.
7. Allow the bread to stand for 5 minutes before removing it from the pan. Turn the bread out onto a cake rack, remove the foil, and let it cool thoroughly before slicing it thin.

RUTHERFORD WYND PUMPKIN BREAD

[MAKES 1 LOAF]

When the leaves turn yellow and orange and a flaming red, it's time to get a can of pumpkin and make this bread. Lovely to share—lovely to be alone with.

8	tablespoons (1 stick) butter, at room temperature
$1^1/_2$	cups sugar
2	eggs
$1^3/_4$	cups sifted all-purpose flour
$^1/_8$	teaspoon baking soda
$1^1/_4$	teaspoons baking powder
$^1/_2$	teaspoon ground cinnamon
$^3/_4$	teaspoon salt
$^1/_2$	teaspoon freshly grated nutmeg
1	cup canned pumpkin
$^1/_4$	cup water, or more as needed
$^1/_2$	cup coarsely chopped pecans or walnuts

1. Preheat the oven to 350°F.

2. Cream the butter and sugar thoroughly in the large bowl of an electric mixer or in a food processor. Add the eggs and continue to beat until the mixture becomes thick and smooth.

3. Resift the flour with the baking soda, baking powder, cinnamon, salt, and nutmeg. Add the flour, pumpkin, and water alternately to the creamed butter and eggs. Do not overbeat. Fold in the nuts with a spatula.

4. Spoon the batter into a lightly greased or foil-lined standard ($9^1/_2$ x $4^1/_2$ x 3-inch) loaf pan. Place the pan on the middle shelf of the oven and bake for about 1 hour. When a skewer inserted into the center comes out dry, the bread is done.

5. Remove the pan from the oven and allow the bread to stand 5 minutes, then turn it out onto a rack. Cool the bread thoroughly before slicing.

TO TOAST NUTS

IN A SKILLET: Toast almonds, whole, sliced, or slivered, in 1 teaspoon of melted butter for each cup of nuts over the lowest possible heat. Toss continuously to prevent burning. Depending on the size of the pieces, almonds will take anywhere from 30 to 35 minutes to toast.

Pine nuts come raw and must always be toasted. Use 1 tablespoon melted butter for each cup of pine nuts. Toast over the lowest possible heat, tossing continuously for 5 minutes. (Pine nuts toast much quicker than almonds.)

IN THE OVEN: Preheat the oven to 300°F. Toast the nuts on a baking sheet until nicely browned. Almonds may take as long as 1 hour; check the pine nuts after 30 minutes.

BREAD

HOMEMADE BREAD

[MAKES 2 LOAVES]

If I were asked which loaf of bread has the definitive traditional flavor of the South, I would say it is this bread. All vegetable shortening can be used, but lard gives the authentic flavor and it does make a delicious crisp crust.

1   package dry yeast

$^1/_4$ cup lukewarm water

6   cups all-purpose flour, sifted

$^1/_4$ cup sugar

$^1/_4$ teaspoon baking soda

$1^1/_4$ teaspoons salt

$^1/_2$ cup lard or solid vegetable shortening, or $^1/_4$ cup lard and $^1/_4$ cup shortening

2   cups buttermilk, or more as needed

1. Dissolve the yeast in the water.
2. Sift 5 cups of the flour with the sugar, baking soda, and salt into a large bowl, or the bowl of an electric mixer or food processor.
3. Cut the lard or shortening into the flour, using a pastry blender or a fork, until it resembles fine meal.
4. Add the dissolved yeast and the buttermilk. (The amount of buttermilk needed will vary—the dough will be sticky but should not be wet.) Blend well.
5. Lift the dough onto a lightly floured surface and knead it heavily, adding enough extra flour to make a firm dough. Knead the dough until the imprint of your fingers pressed hard into the dough remains a few seconds, about 5 minutes.
6. Put the dough in a greased bowl, turning it to coat the surface. Cover the bowl with plastic wrap and leave it in a warm spot until the dough has doubled in bulk, $1^1/_2$ hours.
7. Again, place the dough on a lightly floured surface and knead it well for 2 minutes.
8. Divide the dough in half. Roll out each half to rid it of air bubbles. Roll up each piece of dough as you would a jelly roll, tucking the ends under. Place the loaves into greased standard $9^1/_2$ x $4^1/_2$ x 3-inch) loaf pans.
9. Place the pans in a warm spot, cover them with plastic wrap, and leave them until the dough has again doubled in bulk, 1 hour.
10. Preheat the oven to 425°F.
11. Bake the loaves for 15 minutes. Reduce the heat to 375°F and bake 30 minutes longer. Rap the bread with your knuckle. If it sounds hollow, it is done.
12. Turn the loaves out onto a rack, turning them several times during the cooling process (to keep them crisp).

• To freeze the dough before baking: Allow the dough to rise one time (step 6). Punch it down and knead it for 2 minutes. Roll out the dough, roll it up, and place it in the loaf pans. Cover the pans tightly with foil and freeze them. When you are ready to use the dough, remove the pans from the freezer, uncover, and allow the dough to thaw. When thawed, cover the dough loosely with plastic wrap and let it rise until it has doubled in bulk. Bake as directed. (It usually takes 7 to 8 hours to thaw and rise. I often transfer the frozen loaves to the refrigerator the night before baking. Then it takes about 2 hours at room temperature the next day for the loaves to be ready to bake.)

GREASING THE BOWL

Breads should be left to rise in bowls that have been greased with either solid vegetable shortening or butter. Never use oil—it will soak into the dough—or margarine—it can cause the bread to burn in the baking.

Always turn the dough to coat it with the shortening used to grease the bowl. This will prevent the outer layer of dough from drying out.

SUMMER'S BOUNTY FOR WINTER'S TABLE

Making relishes, chutneys, preserves, and marmalades may come close to a science but it is also an art—a row of those preserved fruits is a beautiful thing.

The late autumn garden is a Southern cook's paradise. It is pickling time. The pepper plants are weighted down with colorful peppers of every size and color. The tiny red ones are the cayenne—hot as _____! We put them in green tomato relishes of every kind, and we dry them for cooking in the winter. The dried ones are the hottest.

The bell peppers—sweet red, green, and yellow—and the true Georgia pimiento are abundant, and we can't preserve them fast enough. They make our pot roasts sing. The Southern watermelons bear late into the autumn. They are not as sweet as the summer melons, but they are divine for watermelon pickles. In October and November the Jerusalem artichokes are ready to be dug, and nothing is better than pickled artichoke with a sweet and tender pork roast or a white meat turkey sandwich.

All winter long you will reap the summer's bounty, and you will be proud. You will have relishes and chutneys for your meat. You will have English muffins, pancakes, and toast with garlands of your finest preserves. Put a bottle of Aunt Nettie's Major Grey Mango Chutney or Fabulous Spiced Green Seedless Grapes under my Christmas tree anytime. They are priceless gems. This chapter is full of gems—read on.

AUNT NETTIE'S MAJOR GREY MANGO CHUTNEY

[MAKES 16 PINTS]

This is a true Madras Indian chutney from Aunt Nettie's collection. Aunt Nettie lived and cooked all over the world, and this is her prize recipe. In the world of mango chutneys, it has no peer. It must be made with mangoes, and it keeps best when frozen; however, when properly processed, it will keep well on the shelf. The recipe can be cut in half successfully.

VARIATION

Add 1 to 2 pounds blanched whole almonds to the chutney 3 minutes or so before removing from the heat (step 5).

10	pounds underripe mangoes
1	pound fresh ginger, peeled and finely chopped, or 1 pound crystallized ginger, finely chopped
1	pound seedless raisins, ground
1	pound currants
2	heads garlic, cloves separated, peeled, and cut in half
5	large red bell or pimiento peppers, cored, seeded, and slivered
6	cinnamon sticks
2	quarts cider vinegar
$1/4$	cup ground ginger
$1/4$	cup cayenne pepper
$1/4$	cup un-iodized salt
8	pounds sugar

If the chutney is kept refrigerated or frozen, the processing is unnecessary; but if the chutney is stored on the shelf, the processing is necessary.

1. Peel the mangoes, slice the flesh from the pits, and cut the flesh into rather thick slices. (The fruit must be underripe.)
2. Put all the ingredients except the sugar into a heavy 8-quart preserving pan.
3. Caramelize the sugar slightly: Put half of the sugar in a large heavy iron skillet over medium heat. When the sugar starts to melt, start stirring. Stir constantly until the sugar has turned a very light amber. Remove from the stove.
4. Add all the sugar to the other ingredients and stir thoroughly to dissolve it. Bring the mixture to a low boil, stirring frequently. This mixture sticks and burns easily—watch it carefully. Place it over a "flame-tamer" if the pan is not a very heavy one.
5. Cook until the mixture has cooked low and the flavors have blended, $2^{1}/_{2}$ to 3 hours. Remove the cinnamon sticks. Pour the chutney into hot sterilized jars (see page 192) to $^{1}/_{4}$ inch from the top of each jar. Seal at once. Process in a boiling-water bath (see page 193) for 5 minutes.

PICKLED PEACHES

[MAKES 6 PINTS]

Clingstone peaches are the best for pickling, but freestones can also be used. The quality of the peaches is the important thing: They should be firm and perfect, with no brown or soft spots. The sugar is added in small amounts to prevent the fruit from hardening and shriveling. Pickled Peaches are one of the great favorites of the South.

4	quarts (about 24) firm, barely ripe peaches
3	pieces dried ginger or about 2 ounces peeled fresh ginger
2	cinnamon sticks
1	tablespoon whole allspice
1	tablespoon whole cloves
6	cups sugar
2	cups water
3	cups cider vinegar

1. Dip the peaches in boiling water for 1 to 2 minutes and then slip off the skins.
2. Tie the ginger, cinnamon, allspice, and cloves in a cheesecloth bag.
3. Combine 2 cups of the sugar, the water, vinegar, and spice bag in a large stainless-steel or enamel pan. Bring the mixture to a boil and simmer about 5 minutes.
4. Add the peaches, a few at a time, to the boiling marinade and allow them to cook until they are tender, about 5 minutes. Remove each batch with a slotted spoon and place it in a large bowl.
5. When all the peaches have been cooked, pour the boiling syrup, with the spice bag, over them. Cover the bowl and allow the peaches to stand in a cool place overnight.
6. The next day, using a slotted spoon, transfer the peaches to hot sterilized jars (see page 192).
7. Pour the syrup, with the spice bag, into a saucepan, add the remaining sugar, and boil until the sugar has dissolved, about 5 minutes. Discard the spice bag and pour the hot syrup over the peaches to $1/4$ inch from the top of each jar. The fruit must be completely covered with the syrup or it will become discolored. Seal at once. Process in a boiling-water bath (see page 193) for 10 minutes. Store in a cool, dark place.

- If the syrup has boiled away too rapidly and there is not enough to cover the peaches, make up half of the recipe of sugar, water, spices, and vinegar. Boil until slightly thickened, 5 to 8 minutes, and pour over the peaches.

SMALL BATCHES

Cooking and preserving in small batches is a wise procedure. Preserves and jellies cook much better in small lots, and you can learn the ways and flavors of the different fruits before it is too late and your sugar bill has gone out of bounds. Easy does it.

Because water processing ruins the flavor and texture of many fruit preserves, cooking in small batches permits you the choice of storing the extra pint or two in the freezer while you enjoy the first. Freezing will keep the preserves safe from bacterial growth, and tasty, too.

If you give any of the frozen or refrigerated preserves to your friends or relatives as gifts, be sure to write on the label that it must be refrigerated immediately to ensure safe eating.

CHECKPOINTS FOR FREEZING

1. Sterilize the freezer jars, screw bands, if using, new lids, and all equipment that will come in contact with the foods or jars (see page 192). 2. Pack the foods into the jars as solidly as possible. Leave enough head space (check recipes) for the food to expand upon freezing. 3. When the jars have cooled, freeze as quickly as possible. 4. Because frozen food gradually deteriorates (the lower the freezer temperature, the slower the deterioration), freeze only what you can use in a reasonable amount of time. 5. The optimum method for thawing frozen food is to let it thaw slowly in the refrigerator overnight.

LATE SUMMER RELISH

[MAKES 4 PINTS]

When the late green tomatoes in the garden begin to turn whitish, they will not be as pretty when canned as the deep green ones. Serve this relish with beef or pork roast, short ribs, beef stews, and dried beans.

4	cups thinly sliced green tomatoes
2	cups thinly sliced red bell or pimiento peppers
2	cups thinly sliced green bell peppers
1	cup thinly sliced onions
$^1/_4$	cup un-iodized salt
4	cups distilled white vinegar
1	cup sugar
2	teaspoons mustard seeds
2	teaspoons celery seeds
1	teaspoon freshly ground white pepper or $^1/_2$ fresh small chile pepper, seeded and slivered

1. Mix the vegetables with the salt in a large bowl. Allow them to stand overnight, covered, in a cool place. The refrigerator is best.
2. The next morning, drain the vegetables thoroughly, pressing them down hard to extract as much juice as possible.
3. Pour the vinegar into a large saucepan and add the sugar and spices. Bring to the boiling point and add the vegetables. Bring to a hard boil and allow the vegetables just to heat through but not to cook. (You want to retain the color and crispness of the vegetables.)
4. Spoon the hot mixture into hot sterilized jars (see page 192), covering the vegetables with the liquid to $^1/_4$ inch from the top of each jar. Seal at once.

VARIATION

- The ingredients may be coarsely chopped or minced instead of sliced.
- A small amount of extra vinegar may be added, if needed, to cover the vegetables in the jars.

FAYETTE COUNTY CHOW-CHOW

[MAKES ABOUT 8 PINTS]

This is a recipe given to me years ago by a good friend and excellent cook in Lexington. It is a favorite Kentucky chow-chow, a bit sweeter than most. We like it with warm ham, and roasts, and chicken sandwiches—and with all kinds of beans. In Mississippi they say one has to have chow-chow with black-eyed peas.

3	pounds tiny gherkin cucumbers
3	pounds tiny pickling onions
1 1/2	heads cauliflower, cut into flowerets
2 1/4	cups un-iodized salt
24	small onions
8	large red bell peppers, cored and seeded
12	medium cucumbers
8	cups sugar
2	quarts cider vinegar
1	cup all-purpose flour
1/2	cup dry mustard
3	tablespoons turmeric
1	tablespoon celery seeds
1	tablespoon mustard seeds

1. Put the gherkins, pickling onions, and cauliflower in separate bowls. Add 1/4 cup of the salt to each bowl, and pour in ice water to cover. Leave, loosely covered, in a cool place, preferably the refrigerator, all day or overnight.

2. Chop the small onions, peppers, and cucumbers separately and put them in separate bowls. Add 1/2 cup salt to each and cover with ice water. Leave, loosely covered, in a cool place, preferably the refrigerator, all day or overnight.

3. When you are ready to make the pickles, drain the gherkins, pickling onions, and cauliflower thoroughly. Drain the chopped vegetables.

4. In a heavy stainless-steel or enamel kettle, combine 6 cups of the sugar with 6 cups of the vinegar. Bring to a boil and stir in all of the vegetables, mixing them well.

5. Quickly mix the flour, mustard, and turmeric with the remaining 2 cups of vinegar until it is very smooth. Stir the paste, along with the celery and mustard seeds, into the vegetables and cook until the sauce has thickened and the flour does not taste raw, 3 to 4 minutes. Taste for sweetness. Add up to 2 cups more sugar if desired, but cook it long enough to dissolve it well.

6. Spoon into hot sterilized jars (see page 192) to 1/4 inch from the top of each jar. Seal at once or cool and refrigerate.

STUFFED PRUNES IN SHERRY

[MAKES 1 1/4 PINTS]

Serve as a conserve with chicken salad, ham, or turkey—or for a bite of something delicious anytime. Especially nice on the tea table or served as a dessert garnished with whipped cream. An exquisite gift idea.

1	pound ready-to-eat pitted prunes
1 1/2	cups walnut halves or blanched whole almonds
1 1/2	cups sherry or Madeira

Stuff each prune with a walnut or almond. Put the prunes in a jar and cover with sherry or Madeira — several days in advance of serving, if possible. Refrigerate until ready to serve..

FABULOUS SPICED GREEN SEEDLESS GRAPES

[MAKES 5 PINTS]

This is one of the stars in my collection of relishes. It evolved over years of working with fruits for preserving. The grapes turn a gorgeous deep amber color, and they are heaven with baked fowl, quail, pheasant, ham, chicken salad, or sliced white meat of turkey sandwiches. Unexcelled for the holidays.

5	pounds firm seedless green grapes (small size, thin-skinned, unripe)
6	cups sugar
1	cup cider vinegar
1/2	cup water
2	thin lemon slices, seeded
1	tablespoon broken cinnamon stick
1	tablespoon whole cloves

1. Wash the grapes, pull them from the stems, and cut each grape in half lengthwise. Discard any soft grapes.

2. Place the grapes in a heavy stainless-steel or enamel pan. Add the sugar, vinegar, water, lemon, and spices. Stir well with a wooden spoon and bring to a boil. Reduce the heat and simmer until the grapes have turned a beautiful deep amber and are transparent, 60 to 80 minutes. (When cold, the syrup should be slightly runny, not solid like jelly.)

3. Ladle the boiling hot grapes with their syrup into hot sterilized jars (see page 192) to 1/4 inch from the top of each jar. Seal at once. Or cool and refrigerate. Or ladle the grapes into prepared freezer jars (see page 184), leaving 1-inch head space, cool, and freeze.

PICKING A GRAPE

Use the Thompson green seedless grape—the smaller the better. Do not use the late-harvest large green seedless grapes that have tough skins. The grapes should not have ripened the least bit.

COLONIAL VIRGINIA MINCEMEAT

[MAKES 8 QUARTS]

VARIATION

Ask your butcher for the suet from around the beef kidney, as free of meat as possible. Chill it and then grind it.

Mincemeat for holiday cookies and pies—and all homemade! Yum-yum. Wonderful Christmas gifts from your kitchen. If the yield is too much for your needs, you may cut the recipe in half.

1	pound light brown sugar
2	pounds granulated sugar
2	pounds beef kidney suet, ground
2	large lemons
2	large navel oranges
1/2	pound candied citron
1/4	pound candied lemon peel
1/4	pound candied orange peel
3	pounds seeded raisins
1	pound seedless raisins
3	pounds currants
1 1/2	teaspoons uniodized salt
1	tablespoon ground cinnamon
1	tablespoon freshly grated nutmeg
1 1/2	teaspoons ground mace
1	teaspoon ground ginger
1/2	teaspoon ground cloves
3	pounds tart apples, peeled, cored, and chopped
4	cups brandy
1	cup aged bourbon whiskey

1. In a large kettle, combine the brown sugar, all but 1 cup of the granulated sugar, and the suet.
2. Cut the colored peel from the lemons and oranges and grind it with 1 cup sugar in a food processor until finely grated. (Or if desired, grate the lemons and oranges by hand.) Add the peel and sugar to the suet.
3. Squeeze the juice from the lemons and oranges. Strain and add the juice to the suet.
4. Chop the citron, candied lemon peel, and candied orange peel in a food processor or by hand, and add them to the suet.
5. Add both raisins and the currants, salt, spices, and apples.
6. Add the brandy and bourbon, and mix thoroughly. Do not cook.
7. Spoon the mincemeat into hot sterilized large jars (see page 192) and seal. The mincemeat will age better when stored in large amounts.

SWEET TEMPTATIONS

Southerners really do have a sweet tooth, and I am among the most guilty. I adore desserts—ice creams, sherbets, pies, puddings, cookies, cakes, and candies—the entire collection.

Grandfather William Irvin Hamby, who was known as Colonel Hamby, said that ice cream was the perfect dessert. Grandfather had been an aide-de-camp of General Nathan Bedford Forrest during the Civil War. He kept the visitors to his spa and all of his family glued to his side for hours on end listening to stories of the war—always with a very sly account of "his" bravery.

But back to the ice cream. During the hot summer days, the hand-cranked ice-cream freezers were turning all the time for the hotel and the soda fountain. Vanilla was the leader, pure, rich, and wonderful.

Considering all the wonderful things we make in our home kitchens, cookies, cakes, and pies are possibly the most amazing, as we start with such simple ingredients: butter, sugar, flour, eggs, milk, and flavorings. In an hour or so they are transformed into a gorgeous two-layered cake, soft and yummy, or maybe cookies so crisp and good they could be called melt-aways because they vanish so fast.

During the long cold days of winter at the hotel, we had glorious puddings or some kind of pie every day. But I have to agree with Grandfather—ice cream is a perfect dessert.

CAMILLE'S GOLDEN COINTREAU CAKE

[SERVES 12 TO 14]

This is the cake I created when, as a young woman, I catered debutante parties and weddings in Louisville. This cake holds a secret all to itself—it is a magical formula that will fool you. The list of ingredients at first glance seems not unlike most good sponge cakes, but there is a difference. The texture is unusually moist, tender, and diaphanous. This delicacy, in contrast to the elusive, rich frosting, sets the cake apart. It is a gala-occasion cake.

STORING COINTREAU CAKE

This cake keeps for weeks in the wintertime and freezes beautifully anytime. Even the frosting does amazingly well in the freezer, and the frozen slices are quite good served as is with coffee.

8	large eggs
1$\frac{1}{2}$	cups sugar
$\frac{1}{3}$	cup fresh orange juice
1	cup all-purpose flour
1$\frac{1}{2}$	teaspoons Cointreau
$\frac{1}{2}$	teaspoon vanilla extract or cognac vanilla (see page 208)
$\frac{1}{4}$	teaspoon salt
$\frac{1}{2}$	teaspoon cream of tartar
	Classic Buttercream with Cointreau (see page 222)

1. Preheat the oven to 325°F.

2. Separate the eggs. Put the yolks in one large mixing bowl and the whites in another large mixing bowl.

3. Beat the egg yolks with an electric mixer until they have thickened and are smooth. Beat in the sugar slowly, then continue beating until the mixture turns a lighter shade of yellow and is smooth. Add the orange juice and blend thoroughly.

4. Measure the flour, then sift it twice. Sprinkle the sifted flour over the egg yolk mixture and gently fold it in by hand with a whisk or a rubber spatula, or with the electric mixer on a very low speed. Fold in the Cointreau and vanilla.

5. Add the salt to the egg whites and beat until they begin to turn white and foamy. Add the cream of tartar and continue to beat until the egg whites hold a stiff peak but are not dry and grainy, about 4 minutes more.

6. Fold a few spoonfuls of the egg whites into the batter to lighten it. Then add the remaining egg whites to the batter, gently folding them in.

7. Spoon the batter into a 10 x 4$\frac{1}{2}$-inch ungreased angel food cake pan (a tube pan with a removable bottom). The pan should be no more than three-quarters full. Place the cake pan on the middle shelf of the oven and bake until a cake tester inserted into the center of the cake comes out clean, or until the cake springs back at once when lightly touched, about 1$\frac{1}{4}$ hours.

8. Remove the cake from the oven, turn it upside down on the tube pan legs, and allow it to rest overnight before frosting.

9. Loosen the cake with a thin sharp knife and unmold it. Put the cake on a plate or on a flat surface covered with waxed paper or foil. Spread the frosting over the cake.

THE CHOCOLATE FINALE CAKE

[SERVES 6]

Once you have made this little chocolate cake, you will be able to turn it out with the greatest ease. It is incredibly rich, but served in small wedges with a bit of whipped cream it is incredibly delicious.

A thin slice is especially good with raspberry or apricot sherbet, or with fresh strawberries or raspberries.

THE CHOCOLATE FINALE FROSTING

5	ounces dark sweet or semisweet chocolate
2	tablespoons heavy or whipping cream
3	tablespoons butter
1	cognac vanilla (see page 208) or vanilla extract

Heat the chocolate and cream in a double boiler and mix gently until smooth. Remove from the heat and stir in the butter and vanilla.

³/₄	cup sugar
4	large eggs, separated
6	ounces German sweet chocolate
³/₄	cup (1 ¹/₂ sticks) butter
5	level tablespoons all-purpose or cake flour. Sifted
6	tablespoons finely grated almonds, pecans, or hazelnuts
	Tiny pinch of salt
1	teaspoon vanilla extract or cognac vanilla (see page 208)
	The Chocolate Finale Frosting (see sidebar)
	Slivered or grated almonds, for garnish (optional)

1. Preheat the oven to 350°F.
2. Beat the sugar and the egg yolks with an electric mixer until they are creamy yellow.
3. Melt the chocolate and butter in a double boiler over simmering water. Remove from the heat and stir until smooth but still warm. Add to the egg yolk mixture and beat well.
4. Fold the flour and grated nuts into the batter by hand.
5. Beat the egg whites until they are stiff but not dry and grainy. Fold them into the batter, and add the salt and vanilla.
6. Spoon the batter into an 8-inch springform pan that has been greased and dusted with flour and lined with foil. The pan should be no more than three-quarters full. Bake until the outside of the cake is solid and the center is still a bit creamy when tested with a knife, about 35 minutes.
7. Allow the cake to cool before turning it out onto a rack.
8. Spread the frosting over the cake, covering the top and sides well. Sprinkle on the nuts if desired. Place the cake in the refrigerator so the frosting can stiffen, 1 hour, if you can wait that long.

• The cake will fall a bit as it cools, and the center should remain a bit creamy.

LUSCIOUS LEMON FROSTING

Peel of 1 lemon

2³/₄ cups confectioners' sugar, sifted

8   tablespoons (1 stick) butter

1   large egg yolk

    Pinch of salt

2   tablespoons lemon juice,
    or more to taste

1. Sliver the lemon peel and combine it with about 1 cup of the sugar in a food processor. Twirl until the lemon peel is finely grated. (You can, if you prefer, grate the lemon peel by hand and add it to the sugar.) 2. Add the butter to the sugar mixture and blend until the mixture is smooth. 3. Add the egg yolk, salt, remaining sugar, and lemon juice. Blend until the frosting is perfectly smooth. Taste, and add another table-spoon of lemon juice if desired.

This frosting will keep in a covered jar in the refrigerator for several days.

DEEP SOUTH PECAN PIE

[MAKES 1 PIE]

Pecan pie is not a difficult pie to make, but it is rich and rather sweet—so much so that it is at its best when served after a very light meal.

STANDARD PASTRY FOR 1-CRUST PIE (see page 223)

3   large eggs

¹/₂   cup sugar

¹/₂   teaspoon salt

6   tablespoons (³/₄ stick) butter, melted

1   cup dark corn syrup

1   teaspoon vanilla extract or cognac vanilla (see page 208)

1   cup pecan halves

1.   Preheat the oven to 375°F.

2.   Roll out and line a 9-inch pie pan with the pastry. Trim the edge even with the rim of the pan.

3.   Combine the eggs, sugar, slat, butter, corn syrup, and vanilla. Mix thoroughly and fold in the pecans.

4.   Spoon the pecan filling into the pie pan.

5.   Place the pie pan on the lower shelf of the oven and bake until the bottom crust is golden brown and the center of the pie seems well set when the pie is shaken, 45 to 50 minutes. The pie will rise a bit in the center when it is done. Cool and serve.

•   Overcooking can make a pecan pie gummy. Time it carefully.

ROSEMARIES

[MAKES 15 TO 18 COOKIES]

This is one of the most elegant of all cookies, and the homemade candied pineapple makes them very special. If you don't have time to prepare it, use pineapple preserves rather than store-bought candied pineapple. Rosemaries are at their best the day they are baked, but they can be frozen unbaked, and then baked as you need them. Oh, the flavor of freshly baked cookies!

TIMING

If you wish to prepare Rosemaries ahead, make them up through step 5 and freeze them in the pans. Then bake them on the day of the party. If baked frozen, they will, of course, require a longer baking period. Allow 25 to 30 minutes.

3	tablespoons pineapple preserves or small chunks of homemade candied pineapple (recipe follows)
8	tablespoons (1 stick) butter, cut into pieces
1/3	cup sugar
1	large egg yolk
1	cup sifted all-purpose flour
1	teaspoon vanilla extract or cognac vanilla (see page 208)

1. At least 3 days ahead, prepare the homemade candied pineapple if you are using it.
2. Cream the butter and sugar thoroughly with an electric mixer until fluffy. Add the egg yolk and beat again. Add the flour and vanilla, and blend well.
3. Wrap the dough in foil and refrigerate to allow it to firm up, at least 20 minutes.
4. Preheat the oven to 325°F.
5. Pinch off small balls of dough, about 1 scant teaspoon each. Place them on a lightly greased or nonstick baking sheet 2 inches apart and press each ball slightly to flatten it. Make a small indentation in the center of each cookie and spoon in 1/2 teaspoon pineapple preserves or press on a small chunk of candied pineapple.
6. Place the cookies on the middle shelf of the oven and bake only until light golden brown, 20 to 25 minutes. They must not be allowed to get very brown. Cool the cookies on a rack.

CANDIED PINEAPPLE

[MAKES ABOUT 1 1/2 CUPS]

1	can (4 ounces) pineapple rings or chunks
3	tablespoons light corn syrup

1. Drain the pineapple thoroughly, reserving the juice. Cut the pineapple into small pieces.
2. Combine the corn syrup and 1/2 cup of the pineapple juice in a medium-size heavy stainless-steel or enamel saucepan. Bring to a boil and cook until the syrup spins a thread, 5 minutes. Add the pineapple and simmer until the fruit is transparent, 35 to 40 minutes.
3. Remove the pan from the heat, cover it loosely with foil, and allow the pineapple to stand overnight.

4.   Return the pineapple and syrup to a boil and cook, spooning the syrup over the pineapple, 2 minutes.

5.   Place a clean piece of muslin or cheesecloth over a cake rack in a warm, sunny room. Remove the pieces of pineapple with a slotted spoon and place them on the cloth. Leave them there until they are almost dry, $1^1/_2$ to 2 days.

6.   Remove the pineapple pieces from the cloth and place them on a piece of heavy foil. Allow them to complete drying at least 1 day. Store between layers of waxed paper or foil in a plastic container. It will keep 4 to 6 weeks at room temperature.

PIE PANS

The advantages of baking 9- or 10-inch pies in heatproof glass pans are twofold: First, you can see through the glass and accurately judge when the crust has browned sufficiently. Second, pie crusts this size bake best in heavy pans. The heat penetrates the crusts more thoroughly, and at the same time the heavier pans hold the heat, resulting in a drier, crisper crust.

Shiny white ceramic pans reflect the heat instead of absorbing it. They are attractive, but they do not bake as efficiently as glass.

WINDFALL APPLE PIE

[MAKES 1 PIE]

Keep a 9-inch skillet or baking dish handy for this fabulously delicious and easy one-crust pie. I call it the Windfall Apple Pie because I make it in the summer with the less-than-perfect apples that fall from the trees in my backyard—the misshapen ones. In the winter I use Granny Smiths, Winesaps, or Golden Delicious from the grocery. In any season, this pie is a glorious windfall.

2	pounds tart apples, peeled and cored
7	tablespoons butter
1/2	cup plus 1 tablespoon sugar
2	tablespoons apple juice, Calvados, brandy, or cider
	Flaky Butter Pastry for 1-crust pie (see page 223)
2	tablespoons heavy or whipping cream

1. Preheat the oven to 425°F.
2. Slice the apples thin. Arrange them in a 9-inch skillet or pan (not black iron). Dot them with the butter and sprinkle with 1/2 cup of the sugar and the chosen liquid.
3. Roll out the pastry and cut it to fit just inside the rim of the pan. Place the pastry over the apples, leaving a small space between it and the edge of the pan.
4. Prick the pastry to allow the steam to escape. Brush it with the cream, and sprinkle it with the tablespoon of sugar (so it will glaze).
5. Bake until the apples are cooked and the crust is golden brown, 30 to 35 minutes.

• Calvados is very delicious in this pie.

MERINGUE

5 large egg whites
Tiny pinch of salt
10 tablespoons sugar

1. Beat the egg whites with the salt until they form a soft peak. 2. Add the sugar gradually, beating until the whites hold a stiff peak.

When stirring the filling as it cooks, go around the sides and bottom of the pan continually, lifting and filling so it will not overcook in spots.

Do not use lime peel in this pie, as it is bitter.

JUPITER ISLAND LIME MERINGUE PIE

[MAKES 1 PIE]

Jupiter Island is a small and beautiful spot on the Indian River in Florida, where I learned of this pie—a great favorite. I think it has a clearer flavor than Key Lime Pie.

STANDARD PASTRY FOR 1-CRUST PIE (see page 223)

3 tablespoons all-purpose flour
1/4 cup cornstarch
1/4 teaspoon salt
1 2/3 cups sugar
2 cups water
5 large egg yolks
2/3 cup fresh lime juice (5 or 6 limes)
2 teaspoons grated lemon peel
Green food coloring (optional)
Meringue (see sidebar)

1. Preheat the oven to 400°F.
2. Roll out and line a 9-inch pie pan with the pastry. Trim the edge even with the rim of the pan. Cover with foil and weight it down with dried beans. Place the pie pan on the bottom rack of the oven and bake about 10 minutes.
3. Remove the beans and the foil, and set the partially baked crust aside to cool.
4. Reduce the oven temperature to 350°F.
5. Mix the flour, cornstarch, and salt with half the sugar in a heavy stainless-steel or enamel saucepan. Add the water and mix well. Bring to a boil and beat constantly with a whisk until the mixture is fairly thick, 3 minutes. Remove from the heat.
6. Beat the egg yolks with the remaining sugar until well mixed. Mix a little of the hot cornstarch mixture into the yolks to temper them. Then add the egg yolk mixture to the remaining cornstarch and sugar. Blend thoroughly. Cook (over direct heat if using enameled iron; if not, over simmering water), stirring constantly, until the filling is quite thick, 3 to 5 minutes. Do not allow it to boil hard. Remove from the heat.
7. Gently blend in the lime juice, lemon peel, and 2 or 3 drops of green food coloring, if desired. Put the filling in the refrigerator to cool and firm up, 6 minutes.
8. Spoon the lime filling into the pie shell. Cover it with the meringue, making sure the meringue covers the filling and seals the edge of the crust (to prevent shrinking and weeping).
9. Place the pie on the middle shelf of the oven and bake until the meringue is light golden brown, 15 to 18 minutes. Watch it carefully.

COGNAC VANILLA

Cut a vanilla bean lengthwise and then crosswise into small pieces, thus exposing the hundreds of black shiny seeds that are the source of the vanilla flavor. Place these cut pieces in a bottle that can be closed airtight. Cover with cognac, brandy, or grain alcohol (2 ounces for 1 vanilla bean), close tightly, and store at room temperature. Shake the bottle well every few days. It will take 2 to 3 weeks for the vanilla to reach its maximum flavor. This extract will always have the bouquet of cognac or brandy. (It will never smell like vanilla extract from the grocery, which is often vanillin, an imitation vanilla.) The pure extract made this way has a more exquisite aroma and flavor, and is vastly superior. The true vanilla essence comes out in baking.

BROWN DIAMOND MOUSSE

[SERVES 6 TO 8]

This dessert has beauty, style, and is absolutely delicious. It does sparkle like brown diamonds. Also, it is uncooked—no small virtue.

2	large egg yolks, at room temperature
2	large eggs, at room temperature
6	tablespoons sugar, plus more for the whipped cream
3	tablespoons Jamaican rum
1	tablespoon fresh lemon juice
$1/4$	cup water
1	tablespoon unflavored gelatin
2	cups heavy or whipping cream
	Almond Praline powder and crystals
1	teaspoon vanilla extract or cognac vanilla (see sidebar)

1. Beat the egg yolks and whole eggs in a large mixing bowl with an electric mixer until they are light and fluffy. Add the sugar a little at a time, keeping the mixture airy. Stir in the rum.

2. Combine the lemon juice, water, and gelatin in a heatproof measuring cup. Stir well to dissolve the gelatin. Set the cup in a pan of boiling water (the water should not come more than two-thirds of the way up the cup) and heat it until the gelatin is clear, $1^{1}/_{2}$ minutes. Remove the cup and set it aside to cool a little. Then stir the gelatin into the egg and rum mixture.

3. Whip 1 cup of the cream until it is stiff, and fold it into the egg and rum mixture. Add 3 tablespoons praline powder and mix.

4. Pour the mousse into a $1^{1}/_{2}$-quart soufflé dish or a pretty glass bowl. Refrigerate for several hours until firm. (Place the bowl in the freezer for about 30 minutes to hasten the process if necessary, but don't allow it to freeze.)

5. Whip the remaining cream, and flavor it with a little sugar and the vanilla. Cover the mousse with the whipped cream and sprinkle it with praline crystals.

CAROLINA FIGS AND RASPBERRIES

The season is all too short for this most elusive, and delicious, combination of fruit. To those with a sensitive palate, it is a real fascination—a connoisseur's dessert.

Serve figs and raspberries plain with a touch of lemon juice, or with cream; or serve them with good crackers and a triple crème cheese or a premium natural cream cheese.

An exquisite finale to any meal.

GLACEED STRAWBERRIES

[SERVES 6]

These charming strawberries for garnishing desserts are as appreciated today as they were in Queen Victoria's day—maybe more so, as we no longer take them for granted.

1	quart perfect large strawberries
2	cups sugar
$^2/_3$	cup water
$^1/_4$	teaspoon cream of tartar
	Tiny pinch of salt
$^1/_2$	teaspoon vanilla extract or cognac vanilla (see page 208)

1. Leave the strawberries' green hulls intact. Rinse the berries and dry them carefully on paper towels.

2. Combine the remaining ingredients in a heavy saucepan. Bring to a boil and cook, without stirring, until a candy thermometer registers 300°F (a little syrup dropped in cold water will thread), 15 minutes. Remove the pan from the heat and place it in a pan of cold water for a few minutes to stop the cooking. Then place the saucepan over boiling water to keep the syrup from hardening.

3. Dip each strawberry up to the hull in the hot glazing syrup. Place the berries on foil. They will cool quickly. Serve in a pretty little basket as a treat after an important meal. (The berries will not remain crisp very long, so glaze them at the last possible minute.)

All sherbets or ices may be poured into a large flat container and placed in the freezing unit for a quicker freezing, if time is of the essence. When frozen, transfer to a bowl for beating.

WATERMELON & RASPBERRY SHERBET

[MAKES 1 ½ QUARTS]

One can seldom get watermelons cold enough, so watermelon sherbet is a good solution. The watermelon used for sherbet must be full-flavored or the sherbet will not be worth the effort. The counterpoint in the flavor of watermelon and raspberry is one you must not miss, as these miracles of taste don't come along very often. Try filling a watermelon shell with sherbet. Very pretty—and most refreshing.

1 ¼ cups sugar

1 ⅛ cups water

3 cups watermelon purée, strained (½ large watermelon)

1 cup fresh or frozen raspberries (thawed), puréed and strained (¼ cup juice)

3 tablespoons fresh lemon juice, or more to taste

1. Combine the sugar and water in a saucepan and boil until clear, 2 minutes. Refrigerate to chill.
2. Mix the sugar syrup with the watermelon and raspberry purées and the lemon juice. Cover with plastic wrap and chill thoroughly. Freeze in an ice-cream freezer following the manufacturer's directions (which is best). Or place the mixture in the freezer, 8 hours or overnight; when it is frozen, beat with an electric mixer until fluffy. Freeze again until firm, another 2 to 3 hours, or you can leave it overnight.

NEW ORLEANS PRALINE ICE CREAM

[MAKES ABOUT 1 GALLON]

Pecan praline in any form is typical of New Orleans, and all the Southern states where the pecan prospers. The praline technique originated in France and Italy, but they, of course, used their native nuts—almonds and hazelnuts. The pecans lend their own unique flavor to praline, and it is redolent of gay and historic New Orleans.

$3/4$ cup sugar

1   cup water

$1/8$ teaspoon cream of tartar

6   large egg yolks

2   cups milk

   Pecan Praline powder (see sidebar)

1   tablespoon cognac, brandy, or praline liqueur

$1^1/2$ teaspoons vanilla extract or cognac vanilla (see page 208)

1   quart heavy or whipping cream

1.   Combine the sugar, water, and cream of tartar in a heavy saucepan. Cook over medium heat until the syrup spins a thread or registers 234°F on a candy thermometer, 7 to 10 minutes.

2.   In the meantime, beat the egg yolks with an electric mixer until they have turned a lighter shade of yellow and are smooth.

3.   Gradually pour the hot syrup into the egg yolks, beating constantly. Pour the egg yolk mixture into a large heavy saucepan. Add the milk and cook over medium heat until the mixture forms a light custard, 8 to 10 minutes. Add the praline powder and blend well.

4.   Pour the mixture into a cool bowl, cover with plastic wrap, and refrigerate at once, $1^1/2$ hours. Allow the mixture to become thoroughly chilled.

5.   When you are ready to make the ice cream, blend the praline custard, chosen liqueur, vanilla, and cream. Freeze in an ice-cream freezer following the manufacturer's directions.

6.   Serve in sherbet glasses garnished with praline pecan halves.

PECAN PRALINE

[MAKES $3/4$ CUP]

$3/4$ cup sugar

$1/3$ cup water

$1/4$ teaspoon cream of tartar

1   cup pecan halves

1. Combine the sugar, water, and cream of tartar in a heavy skillet. Cook over medium heat, stirring a bit, until the sugar has completely melted and has turned a rich golden brown. 2. In the meantime, butter a heavy baking sheet and scatter the pecans on it. 3. The minute the syrup is the right shade of caramel, pour it over the pecans. Cool completely. When the caramel is hard, break it up with a mallet, but reserve a few of the whole pecans to use as a garnish. To make praline powder, put small pieces of praline in a food processor and grind until fine.

THE ULTIMATE VANILLA ICE CREAM

[MAKES ABOUT 3 QUARTS]

This vanilla ice cream is the master recipe for many wonderful ice creams. The custard is one secret to its goodness; when you make the custard, beat the eggs and sugar together until they are creamy. A very light custard, or one that is not allowed to thicken much, will make a delicately flavored ice cream. For an egg-rich flavor, allow the custard to coat the spoon more heavily. A prime ingredient for a very special ice cream is your own homemade cognac vanilla.

6	large egg yolks
3/4	cup sugar
2	cups milk, warmed
	Tiny pinch of salt
2	teaspoons vanilla extract or cognac vanilla (see page 208)
1	quart heavy or whipping cream, chilled

1. Combine the egg yolks and sugar in a large mixing bowl, and beat hard with an electric mixer until the mixture turns a lighter shade of yellow and is creamy. Stir the milk in with a whisk.

2. Cook the mixture in a heavy saucepan over medium heat, or in the top of a double broiler over simmering water, until the custard coats a wooden spoon nicely, 8 to 10 minutes.

3. Pour the custard into a cool bowl (stainless steel is excellent), cover with plastic wrap, and refrigerate at once. Allow it to become thoroughly chilled, about 1 1/2 hours.

4. When you are ready to make the ice cream, add the salt and vanilla to the custard. Combine it with the cream and blend thoroughly. Freeze in an ice-cream freezer following the manufacturer's directions.

VANILLA BEANS

When I was young, vanilla beans (still in their outer brownish shells) were so cheap they were shipped in burlap sacks from Mexico. My father had the outer coat shelled from the beans, and then the black, moist bean itself was cut and marinated in grain alcohol. It was stored in chemical bottles (I can see them now) to be used in making ice creams and chocolate and fruit syrups for the soda fountain—Dawson Springs Salts and Water Company—next to our hotel. They knew no other way, and little did they realize the superiority of their product.

ENGLISH CUSTARD SOUFFLÉ

[SERVES 6]

This is a very and flavorful soufflé—a delight to all those who are devoted to custard. It has no fruit or nuts to weight it down and it can rise extremely high.

3	tablespoons butter
3	tablespoons all-purpose flour
1	cup milk
¹/₂	cup plus 3 tablespoons sugar
5	large yolks, at room temperature
6	large egg whites
1¹/₂	teaspoons vanilla extract or cognac vanilla (see page 208), or 1 tablespoon cognac
¹/₄	teaspoon cream of tartar
	Pinch of salt
	Apricot-Almond Sauce, chilled (see sidebar)

1. Preheat the oven to 375°F.

2. Melt the butter over medium heat in a heavy saucepan. Blend in the flour and stir until smooth. Gradually stir in the milk; cook, stirring constantly, until a thick, smooth sauce is formed, 1 minute. Add ¹/₂ cup sugar and beat thoroughly to help dissolve it. Add the egg yolks and beat hard. Set the mixture aside but keep it warm.

3. In a large mixing bowl, combine the egg whites, vanilla or cognac, cream of tartar, and salt. Beat until the egg whites stand in stiff peaks but are not dry and grainy. Gently fold the whites into the egg yolk mixture, leaving some particles of egg white showing.

4. Butter a 6-cup soufflé dish, sprinkle it with the 3 tablespoons of sugar, and fit it with a greased foil collar that extends 2 inches above the rim of the dish. Pour in the soufflé mixture.

5. Place the dish on the middle shelf of the oven and bake for 35 to 40 minutes. Remove the foil collar. Serve hot, with chilled Apricot-Almond Sauce.

APRICOT-ALMOND SAUCE

[MAKES 1³/₄ CUPS]

1¹/₂	cups apricot preserves
¹/₂	cup water
	Tiny pinch of salt
1	tablespoon kirsch or rum, or more to taste
¹/₄	cup slivered blanched almonds

Combine the apricot preserves, water, and salt in a saucepan. Simmer until a syrup is formed and thickens, 7 minutes. Remove from the heat and add the kirsch or rum and the almonds.

SOUR CREAM FUDGE

There is something delightfully human about people who have a nagging sweet tooth. Have you ever noticed how they hide goodies in funny places—in dresser drawers, for instance—away from themselves, of course. Then Valentine's Day comes along and boxes of chocolate are all over the place, right out in the open. Could there ever be a better excuse for candy?

This is a delicious white fudge with a pleasing tang that tastes of lemon. It improves in flavor overnight.

GEORGIA'S GOLDEN BRITTLE

[MAKES $^3/_4$ POUND BRITTLE]

Among the Deep South brittles, this one is as easy as it is elegant. You can make it on the rainiest day. Use your own homemade vanilla and huge pecans—delectable. You'll see!

1$^1/_2$	cups large pecans (the larger the better)
1	cup sugar
$^1/_2$	cup light corn syrup
$^1/_8$	teaspoon cream of tartar
$^1/_8$	cup cold water
	Tiny pinch of salt
2	tablespoons unsalted butter
2	teaspoons brandy or cognac
1$^1/_2$	teaspoons vanilla extract or cognac vanilla (see page 208)

1. Butter a baking sheet, a large heatproof baking dish, or a meat platter measuring about 13$^1/_2$ x 9 inches. Scatter the pecans over the butter.
2. Combine the sugar, corn syrup, cream of tartar, water, and salt in an extra-heavy 1-quart saucepan (unlined copper or enameled iron is excellent). Stir well, bring to a boil, and cook until the mixture reaches the hard crack stage and registers 300°F on a candy thermometer, 15 minutes. Then quickly stir in the unsalted butter.
3. Remove the pan from the heat. Wait a second or two, then stir in the brandy or cognac and the vanilla. Quickly pour the syrup over the pecans. With a wooden spoon, and working fast, toss the pecans about in the syrup to cover them thoroughly, and spread the brittle out thin.
4. Allow the brittle to cool completely. Then break it into rough pieces and store it in a tin.

SOUR CREAM FUDGE

[MAKES 24 SQUARES]

1$^1/_2$	cups sugar
$^1/_2$	cup sour cream
$^1/_8$	teaspoon salt
$^3/_4$	teaspoon vanilla extract or cognac vanilla (see page 208)
1	cup coarsely chopped pecans or walnuts

1. Combine the sugar, sour cream, and salt in a bowl and mix until the sugar is well moistened. Pour the mixture into a heavy saucepan, and put it on a "flame-tamer" over medium heat. From time to time wipe the crystals from the sides of the pan with a damp pastry brush.

2. Cook until a candy thermometer reads 236°F, or a teaspoon of the syrup dropped into cold water forms a soft ball, 10 minutes. Remove the pan from the heat. Wipe any crystals again from the sides of the pan with a damp brush.

3. Cool the fudge to 11°F. Then add the vanilla, and beat with a wooden spoon until the fudge begins to lose its transparency, 5 minutes. Stir in the nuts.

4. Pour the fudge onto a buttered marble slab or a buttered baking sheet measuring about 12 x 9 inches. Cool completely, then cut into squares. Store in a tight tin box.

DESSERTS

COINTREAU FROSTING

8 tablespoons (1 stick) unsalted butter, cut into pieces

3³/₄ cups confectioners' sugar, sifted

¹/₈ teaspoon salt

1 large egg yolk

6 – 8 tablespoons Cointreau, or more as needed

1. Put the butter in a large mixing bowl. Add the confectioners' sugar and salt. Beat well with an electric mixer. Add the egg yolk, then slowly add 6 tablespoons of the Cointreau. Continue to beat the frosting until it is smooth, thick, and pliable, 3 minutes. Add more Cointreau as needed; it usually takes at least 8 tablespoons. This frosting must be thick.

2. Frost the cake generously in a swirl design. Allow the frosting to firm for 30 minutes, then lift the cake to a serving platter.

CLASSIC BUTTERCREAM WITH COINTREAU

1 cup (2 sticks) unsalted butter, cut into pieces

5 large egg yolks

²/₃ cup sugar

¹/₄ teaspoon cream of tartar

¹/₈ teaspoon salt, or to taste

5 tablespoons cold water

3 tablespoons Cointreau

1. Cream the butter until it is light and smooth. Set aside.

2. Beat the egg yolks with an electric mixer until thy have doubled in bulk, 3 minutes.

3. Combine the sugar, cream of tartar, salt, and water in a heavy saucepan, bring to a boil, and cook over medium heat until the syrup spins a thread when it falls from a wooden spoon or until a candy thermometer registers 235° to 236°F. (If the syrup is not cooked to this point, the buttercream will never firm up.)

4. Immediately pour the hot syrup in a steady stream into the egg yolks, beating constantly. Continue to beat until the mixture has cooled, 15 to 20 minutes.

5. Add the butter to the yolk mixture a tablespoonful at a time. If the frosting should look curdled while you are adding the butter, place the frosting over hot (not boiling) water and beat vigorously until it is smooth again. Add the Cointreau and mix thoroughly. If necessary, chill the frosting until it has a good spreading consistency, 35 to 45 minutes.

6. Frost the cake generously in a beautiful swirling design, and then keep the cake refrigerated.

FLAKY BUTTER PASTRY

[MAKES 2 CRUSTS]

This Flaky Butter Pastry is the quintessential butter pastry of all so-called pie crusts. It does not rank second to puff pastry. It stands alone. It has a versatility very few crusts have. It is by far the easiest of all crusts to blend and to roll, and the flavor is unsurpassed. This is the pastry I teach first to a new student, and it always remains a favorite. It flakes, and it melts in one's mouth. A most divine crust for apple, rhubarb, peach, or strawberry pie.

The recipe makes enough for a 2-crust pie. See the Variation for the amounts needed to make just 1 crust.

2¹/₄ cups (11 ounces) sifted all-purpose flour

³/₄ teaspoon salt

14 tablespoons (1³/₄ sticks) butter, chilled and cut into pieces

¹/₃ cup ice water, or as needed

1. Sift the flour and salt into a mixing bowl. Cut the butter into the flour with a pastry blender until the mixture resembles coarse meal.

2. Sprinkle on the ice water a little at a time, blending it quickly into the dough by gathering up the mixture, working it lightly with your fingers, then squeezing it together. (Work fast, as the mixture must stay cold.) The dough should be soft enough to easily form into a ball. If it isn't, add a little more water.

3. Form the dough into a ball. Cut it in half and roll each half out at once on a lightly floured surface or pastry cloth. (Or cover with foil and refrigerate until ready to use.)

4. As soon as it has been rolled out, fit the bottom crust into the pie pan. Then it can be covered and refrigerated or frozen until ready to use. Roll out the top crust, place it on a waxed paper-lined baking sheet, cover with foil, and refrigerate or freeze until ready to use.

VARIATION

• For a 1-crust pie: Use 1 cup plus 2 tablespoons (5^1/$_2$ ounces) flour, a pinch of salt, 7 tablespoons butter, and about ^{1}/$_4$ cup ice water. This will give you a little extra pastry dough, but don't try to change the proportions. Use the extra to make turnovers or toast fingers.

STANDARD PASTRY

[MAKES 2 CRUSTS]

This is the classic American pie crust. It is made with vegetable shortening, which is a hard fat, so it is not as easy to blend or roll as a butter pastry, but it is more economical and not as rich. There are certain times when this is the perfect pastry for that very reason. For instance, pecan pie and several other Southern pies that are on the sweet side need the blandness of the vegetable-shortening crust. (Lard, which has been used in the South for pastry for several hundred years, does make a lovely, crisp crust, but vegetable shortening is excellent and more in favor today.)

This recipe is for a 2-crust pie. See the Variation for the amounts needed to make a 1-crust pie.

2 cups sifted all-purpose flour

1 teaspoon salt

^{2}/$_3$ cup solid vegetable shortening, chilled

6 – 8 tablespoons ice water

1. Sift the flour and salt together in a mixing bowl. Cut the vegetable shortening into the flour with a pastry blender until the mixture resembles coarse meal.

2. Sprinkle on the ice water a little at a time, blending it quickly into the dough by gathering up the mixture, working it lightly with your fingers, then squeezing it together. Form the dough into a ball. Cut the ball in half and roll out the bottom crust at once on a lightly floured surface or pastry cloth. (Or, if desired, wrap the dough in foil and refrigerate it until you are ready to use it; but rolling it out at once is easier.)

3. As soon as the dough has been rolled out, fit the bottom crust into the pie pan. Then it can be covered and refrigerated or frozen. Roll out the top crust, place it on a waxed paper-lined baking sheet, cover with foil, and refrigerate or freeze until ready to use.

VARIATION

• For a 1-crust pie: Use 1^1/$_2$ cups flour, ^{3}/$_4$ teaspoon salt, ^{1}/$_2$ cup chilled vegetable shortening, and 3 to 6 tablespoons ice water.

If the pastry feels hard and is difficult to roll, you didn't use enough water. If the pastry is as soft as biscuit dough and is tough when baked, you used too much.

Pastry dough must be kept cold or it will not be flaky.

HOW TO ROLL OUT PASTRY

1. Make up the dough for a 2-crust pie and divide it in half. Wrap one half in foil and refrigerate it.

2. Place the other half of the dough on a lightly floured surface. Flatten it a bit with a rolling pin. Then roll lightly from the center to the edge, lifting the rolling pin on each stroke as it nears the edge. Always roll from the center out, forming a circle large enough to extend 1 inch over the edge of the pie pan. Roll the pastry thin—never more than ^{1}/$_8$ inch thick. The bottom crust should be even less than ^{1}/$_8$ inch thick, if possible.

3. Roll the pastry up on the rolling pin. Lift it over the center of the pie pan and unroll. With your fingers, fit the pastry loosely into the pie pan. (This helps keep the dough from shrinking below the edge of the pan.)

4. Fill the pastry as desired.

5. Roll the second half of the dough exactly as you did the first. Roll it up loosely on the rolling pin, center it over the pie, and unroll.

6. Moisten the bottom edge of the pie crust with water, then press the top and bottom edges together. Trim off the excess dough with scissors. Fold the edges of the crusts under the rim of the pie plate, pressing them together firmly.

7. Make a few slits in the top crust with a sharp knife to allow the steam to escape.

8. Press the edges down around the rim of the pie plate with the tines of a fork, or flute. Bake as directed.

TO FLUTE

Place your right index finger on the inside rim of the pastry, your left index finger and thumb outside. Press together and work around the rim to form a fluted rim. The fluted edge has a greater tendency to overbrown than do pastry edges that are pressed flat with the tines of a fork.

BRUNCH IS AT ELEVEN...

Brunch is at eleven,

Punch is at three,

Coffee is at seven,

But where's my tea?

I love brunch. One of its great charms is the time of day—eleven to twelve or thereabout. The early morning rush has subsided by then, the plans for the day are lined up, and we suddenly find ourselves very hungry. We welcome good food at that point, and the chance to enjoy it in peace, if only for a few moments.

If you are entertaining, brunch is easier than a luncheon. One main dish is enough, and it can be very special or it can be very simple, such as fresh fruit juice and Sour Cream Pancakes with blueberries, or an omelet with fresh herbs or sautéed ham, and hot biscuits with your best preserves. If you have just come from picking strawberries, have those. Call up your friend, especially if she grew up north of the Mason-Dixon line, and invite her over for brunch. Sit her down with a cup of Spiced Tea. Then you say, "Now I will show you what a real strawberry shortcake tastes like." That will be fun.

SPINACH AND HAM FILLING

4   tablespoons (¹/₂ stick) butter

2   tablespoons all-purpose flour

1   cup milk

    Salt and freshly ground black
    pepper to taste

2   shallots, finely chopped (optional)

3   tablespoons water (optional)

¹/₂   pound mushrooms, chopped

1   cup freshly cooked chopped spinach
    (1 pound uncooked), well drained

¹/₂   cup slivered baked ham

1. Melt 2 tablespoons of the butter in a
heavy saucepan. Add the flour and blend
until smooth. Slowly add the milk and
cook, stirring constantly, until the mixture
is thick and smooth, about 5 minutes.
Season with salt and pepper. Keep warm.
2. Melt the remaining butter in a skillet.
If using shallots, add the shallots and the
water, and sauté over medium heat until
the water has boiled away. Add the mushrooms and sauté until they give up their
moisture, keeping them somewhat crisp,
about 1 minute. 3. Combine the shallots
and mushrooms, spinach, and ham with
the cream sauce. Taste for seasoning and
correct if necessary. Keep warm until you
are ready to fill the omelet.

ROLLED OMELET SOUFFLÉ

[SERVES 4 TO 6]

This rolled omelet is easier than it sounds, and it is spectacular. It will hold in a warm oven for an hour, believe it or not. And the variations are fun.

4   tablespoons (¹/₂ stick) butter

¹/₂   cup all-purpose flour

¹/₂   teaspoon salt

    Cayenne pepper to taste

2   cups milk

5   large eggs, separated

    Spinach and Ham Filling (see sidebar)

1. Grease a 15¹/₂ x 10¹/₂ x 1-inch jelly roll pan. Line it with waxed paper, and coat the paper too. Set the pan aside.

2. Melt the butter in a heavy saucepan. Add the flour and blend until smooth. Add the salt and cayenne. Slowly pour in the milk, stirring constantly with a whisk, and cook until the mixture has thickened and is smooth again, about 5 minutes.

3. Beat the yolks and add a little of the hot sauce to temper them. Pour the yolk mixture into the sauce and cook over medium heat a minute more. Do not allow it to boil. Set the mixture aside to cool.

4. While the mixture is cooling, prepare the filling.

5. Preheat the oven to 400°F.

6. Beat the egg whites until they are stiff but not dry and grainy. Gently fold them into the cooled mixture and spread it out in the prepared pan. Place the pan in the oven and cook only until well puffed and brown, about 15 minutes. Invert the omelet at once onto a clean towel. Spread it with warm filling and roll it up like a jelly roll.

VARIATIONS

*   Make a filling of all creamed mushrooms, or all ham, or half mushrooms and half ham.
*   Substitute chopped fresh asparagus for the spinach and omit the shallots. Or use a thick, rich tomato sauce instead of the spinach mixture. Season both with fresh or dried tarragon.
*   Substitute 4 slices crisp bacon, chopped, for the ham.

WHOLE-WHEAT WAFFLES

[SERVES 6]

If Whole-Wheat Waffles sound too heavy, these will fool you. They are light and flavorful—and served with Brown Sugar, Cinnamon, and Walnut Syrup, they will brighten the gloomiest day.

1/2	cup all-purpose flour
1 1/2	cups whole-wheat flour
1/2	teaspoon salt
3 1/2	teaspoons baking powder
2	large eggs, separated
1 3/4	cups milk or buttermilk
8	tablespoons (1 stick) butter, melted and cooled
4	tablespoons butter
2	tablespoons vegetable oil

1. Sift the all-purpose flour into a bowl. Add the whole-wheat flour (unsifted), salt, and baking powder, and mix well.

2. Combine the egg yolks, milk or buttermilk, and melted butter in a roomy bowl. Add the flour mixture a little at a time, beating thoroughly with a whisk. (This part can be done with an electric mixer or in a food processor.)

3. Beat the egg whites until they hold a stiff peak but are not dry or grainy. Gently fold them into the flour and egg mixture.

4. Heat the solid butter and the oil in a small saucepan and keep warm. Heat a waffle iron over high heat and brush it with oil and butter before cooking each waffle.

5. Cook until golden brown and serve immediately with your favorite syrup.

• This batter, stored in a covered jar, holds well overnight. It also holds better when made with milk rather than buttermilk.

BROWN SUGAR, CINNAMON, AND WALNUT SYRUP

[MAKES 1 3/4 CUPS]

1	cup loosely packed light brown sugar
1	cup granulated sugar
1/4	cup light corn syrup
2	cups water, or more as needed
1	cinnamon stick (2 inches)
3	tablespoons butter
1 1/2	tablespoons finely chopped walnuts or pecans

1. Combine the sugars in a heavy saucepan. Add the corn syrup, water, and cinnamon stick. Simmer until a syrup has formed, 10 to 12 minutes. Add a little more water if the syrup becomes too thick. 2. Discard the cinnamon stick and add the butter and nuts. Simmer a minute and serve warm.

The corn syrup is used to help prevent the syrup from crystallizing. If the syrup should crystallize upon standing, add a little water and lemon juice, or a pinch of cream of tartar, and boil again for a few minutes.

SOUR CREAM PANCAKES

[SERVES 6]

This is an all-time favorite sour cream. The superb batter can be used in any number of ways with berries and fruit sauces, but blueberry pancakes are hard to beat. In the wintertime, make the Sour Cream Pancakes plain and serve them with the sauce made with frozen blueberries.

$1^1/2$ cups all-purpose flour

Pinch of salt

$2^1/2$ teaspoons baking powder

$^1/4$ teaspoon baking soda

1 teaspoon sugar

2 large eggs

6 tablespoons ($^3/4$ stick) butter, melted

$^2/3$ cup sour cream

$^2/3$ cup milk

1 cup blueberries, currants, or raspberries

4 tablespoons ($^1/2$ stick) butter

2 tablespoons vegetable oil

Confectioners' sugar, for dusting

Blueberry Sauce (see sidebar)

1. Combine the flour, salt, baking powder, baking soda, and sugar.

2. Beat the eggs in a roomy bowl until fluffy. Add the melted butter, sour cream, and milk.

3. Add the dry ingredients to the egg mixture and beat well. Fold the berries in gently so they will not bleed.

4. Heat the solid butter and the oil in a small saucepan and keep warm. Heat a griddle or skillet over high heat, and brush it with the oil and butter before cooking each batch of pancakes. Pour 2 to 3 tablespoons batter for each pancake onto the griddle or skillet. When the underside is golden brown, turn the pancake.

5. To serve, sift confectioners' sugar over the top and pass the warm Blueberry Sauce.

- This is a rather thick batter; it makes a cakelike but tender pancake. For a thinner pancake, add $^1/4$ cup more milk.
- If not serving Blueberry Sauce with the pancakes, increase the berries to $1^1/2$ cups.

BLUEBERRY SAUCE

$^2/3$ cup sugar, or to taste

2 tablespoons cornstarch

Pinch of salt

$1^1/2$ cups water

2 cups fresh blueberries

2 tablespoons butter, melted

2 tablespoons fresh lemon juice

$^1/2$ teaspoon grated lemon peel

Mix the sugar and cornstarch together in a medium saucepan. Add the salt, water, berries, and melted butter. Cook, stirring often, over medium heat until the sauce has thickened and is clear, 20 to 25 minutes. Add the lemon juice and peel, stir, and serve.

This sauce can be made with other berries, but blueberries seem to be the favorite.

INDIAN RIVER ORANGE & LEMON PANCAKES

[SERVES 4]

Glorious breakfasts are full of surprises. How good to be in Florida for a while and have these orange pancakes. They blend with all kinds of yummy syrups and preserves.

$^1/_2$	navel orange
$^1/_2$	lemon
3	tablespoons sugar
4	large eggs
$^1/_2$	teaspoon salt
1	cup heavy or whipping cream or sour cream
1	tablespoon lemon juice, or to taste
1	cup sifted all-purpose or cake flour
2	teaspoons baking powder
4	tablespoons ($^1/_2$ stick) butter
2	tablespoons vegetable oil

WHIPPING CREAM

If you use heavy or whipping cream, beat it gently in step 2; it must not whip. If you use sour cream, you may want an extra tablespoon of sugar. The sweet cream is best.

1. Cut the peels from the orange and lemon into thin slivers. Combine the peels and sugar in a food processor and twirl until the peels are finely grated. (Or you can grate the peels by hand and combine them with the sugar.)
2. Put 1 whole egg and 3 egg yolks (reserve the whites) in the bowl of an electric mixer or in the processor. Gradually beat in the sugar, then continue beating until the mixture falls like a ribbon when dropped from a spoon. Add the salt, heavy cream or sour cream, and lemon juice, and mix.
3. Blend in the flour and baking powder with a whisk.
4. Beat the egg whites until stiff, then fold them into the batter.
5. Heat the butter and oil in a small saucepan and keep warm. Heat a griddle or skillet over high heat, and brush it with the oil and butter before cooking each batch of pancakes. Cook the pancakes promptly. Serve with your favorite syrup, jelly, preserves, or marmalade.

THE BEST OF MINT JULEPS

It has long been debated whether the mint julep belongs to Virginia or Kentucky, but we think Kentucky has an edge on the controversy. There are a myriad of recipes for this traditional Southern drink, but Henry Watterson, the famous editor of the Courier-Journal two generations ago, can still stand as the ultimate authority on the best of all mint juleps:

Pluck the mint gently from "its bed, just as the dew of the evening is about to form upon it. Select the choicer sprigs only, but do not rinse them. Prepare the simple syrup, and measure out a half-tumbler of aged bourbon. Pour the whiskey into a well-frosted silver cup full of ice with several sprigs of mint—just to sniff the fragrance. Throw the simple syrup away."

KENTUCKY EGGNOG

[SERVES 20]

Cookies to go with punches must not be overly sweet or rich. Chocolate wafers or nut cookies balance the flavor of a good eggnog.

12	large eggs, separated
1¼	cups sugar, or to taste
1	quart milk, chilled
1	quart heavy or whipping cream, chilled
1	fifth aged bourbon
1	cup cognac or brandy
	Freshly grated nutmeg, for garnish

1. Beat the egg yolks until they are light and fluffy. Add the sugar and continue beating until the sugar has dissolved and the mixture is again light and fluffy. Chill at least 1 hour.

2. Add the milk and cream to the chilled yolks and set over a bowl of ice. Add the bourbon and cognac or brandy very, very slowly (or the eggs will curdle).

3. Beat the egg whites until they are stiff and fold them in. Sprinkle with freshly grated nutmeg.

•   The quality and proof of the bourbon and cognac or brandy do matter. The flavor comes through the eggs and cream just as clearly as in any mixed drink.

•   When making eggnog in smaller batches, allow 1½ to 2 jiggers bourbon and 1½ tablespoons sugar for each egg.

•   All liqueurs and spirits containing alcohol will curdle eggs if they are not added very slowly. The mixture must be kept cold or it will separate.

VARIATION

•   Float whipped cream flavored with Jamaican rum on top of the punch.

THE PALM BEACH COOLER

[SERVES 15]

A beautiful summer cooler for a luncheon or afternoon tea. A fruity California
wine, not too dry, is fine here.

6   thin orange slices, seeded
6   thin lemon slices, seeded
2   cups cubed fresh pineapple
    Sugar to taste
2   bottles white wine, chilled
    Fresh mint, for garnish

1. Combine the orange, lemon, and pineapple in a large bowl. Add sugar to taste.
2. Add the white wine and stir well. Pour
into tall glasses filled with ice, and garnish
with sprigs of mint. Pass the sugar.

SPICED TEA

[SERVES 8]

This is an excellent spiced tea, served hot or cold.

4   cups freshly drawn cold water
4   tea bags
$1/2$ cup fresh orange juice
$1/4$ cup fresh lemon juice
$1/2$ cup sugar, or to taste
3   pieces cinnamon stick, broken
16   whole cloves
6   lemon slices, for garnish

1. Bring the water to a boil, pour it over the tea bags, and steep 5 minutes. Remove the tea bags.
2. Add the fruit juices, sugar, and spices. Keep warm and allow the flavors to ripen about 20 minutes.
3. Bring almost, but not quite, to a boil, and serve, garnished with lemon slices.

•   This recipe may be tripled, but use only $1^1/4$ cups sugar.

AMBER ICED TEA

Pour freshly drawn cold water over 4 to 8 tea bags in a quart jar. Set in the refrigerator at once. Allow to sit 9 to 12 hours, according to the strength you desire. This tea will be clear. It is not as fine a brew as the one made correctly with boiling water, but some people find it easier.

COFFEE PUNCH

[SERVES 30]

A favorite for weddings, anniversaries, and debut parties.

6	cups heavy or whipping cream
4	quarts fresh extra-strong brewed coffee, chilled
5	tablespoons sugar
2	quarts vanilla ice-cream
1	tablespoon vanilla extract

1. Whip 2 cups of the cream.
2. Combine the coffee, sugar, remaining cream, ice-cream, and vanilla. Stir, and garnish with the whipped cream.

VARIATION

• Add 4 to 5 tablespoons brandy or cognac.

VIRGINIA COFFEE SYLLABUB

[SERVES 8]

A Colonial Virginia drink that was served at the Governor's Palace in Williamsburg.

$1\frac{1}{2}$	cups strong brewed coffee, chilled
1	cup heavy or whipping cream
$\frac{1}{2}$	cup milk
1	cup aged bourbon whiskey

1. Combine the coffee, cream, milk, and whiskey in a glass or china mixing bowl. Beat the mixture with a rotary beater until it is well blended. Sweeten to taste, and chill thoroughly, about 1 hour in the freezer.
2. Beat the syllabub again before pouring it into small cups or sherry glasses.

HOT CHOCOLATE

[SERVES 4]

The different brands of semisweet chocolate may vary somewhat in sweetness, so add the sugar to your taste.

3   cups milk

1   cup water

6   ounces semisweet chocolate, coarsely chopped

2   teaspoons sugar

      Whipped cream, for garnish

Combine the milk, water, and chocolate in a heavy saucepan. (The pan must be heavy, to prevent burning; or heat the mixture over hot water or in a double boiler.) Add the sugar and heat until piping hot. Serve garnished with whipped cream.

THE ULTIMATE HOT CHOCOLATE

The taste of orange in Grand Marnier is marvelous with chocolate.

Make Hot Chocolate, but use only 4 ounces semisweet chocolate. Add 1 tablespoon Grand Marnier to each cup of chocolate. Season the whipped cream with a hint of the liqueur. Serve with hot croissants, or your favorite homemade bread, or butter cookies. Live.

PENDENNIS CLUB WEDDING PUNCH

[SERVES ABOUT 40]

Mr. Fred Crawford, the longtime manager of Louisville's Pendennis Club, gave me the recipe for this baroque punch they served at weddings and parties.

$2^{1}/_{4}$ cups fresh lemon juice (12 lemons)

1   quart carbonated water, chilled

$^{1}/_{2}$ pint Cherry Herring

$^{1}/_{2}$ pint Cointreau

1   pint brandy

2   bottles champagne, chilled

1   cup sugar, or to taste

      Fruit in season, for garnish

Just before serving, combine all the ingredients except the fruit. Pour the punch over a block of ice in a punch bowl and garnish with strawberries, slices of orange or lemon, or other fruit.

INDEX

INDEX

INDEX

PHOTO CREDITS

Page 6 courtesy of Antoine's New Orleans.

Pages 186, 198, 238 by Kit Barry.

Page 120 courtesy of the
Cape Fear Museum Photo Department.

Pages 98, 164, 210, courtesy of
Corbis Royalty Free Images.

Page 297 courtesy of the Enoch Pratt
Free Library, Maryland Department.

Pages 50, 64 70, 82, 110, 154,174, 180 184,
206 courtesy of the Florida Department of
State Historical Archives: p. 174, Leonard
Dakin; p. 110, W.A.P. Fishburgh; p. 64,
Miles Womack.

Page 152 courtesy of the
Georgia Department of Archives and History.

Page 150 courtesy of the
Historic New Orleans Collection.

Pages 24, 42, 112, 148, 196, 204 courtesy of
Kentucky Historical Society.

Pages 28, 100, 202 courtesy of the
Lelia Abercrombie Historical Library.

Pages 118, 122 courtesy of the Mariner's
Museum: p. 122, John Frye Collection.

Pages 8, 26, 156 courtesy of the
Maryland Historical Society.

Pages 22, 34, 48, 54, 58, 64, 74,116, 146, 124,
168 182, 188, 220 courtesy of the USDA
Photographic Archives Historical Photos:
Pages 74, 188, USDA History Collection,
National Agricultural Library special collections.

Page 10, 21, 30, 44, 52, 72, 88, 96, 114, 138,
140, 162, 166, 172, 212, 218, 236, 239
courtesy of the University of Louisville
Photographic Archives: p. 72, 138, 172, 239,
R. G. Potter Collection; p. 96, 218, Bradley
Collection; p. 21, Cooper Collection; p. 212,
Ford Collection; p. 10, 44, 52, 80, 88, 162,
166, Caufield and Shook Collection; p. 140,
Royal Photo Studio Collection; p. 114,
Griswold Collection; p. 30, Standard Oil
(New Jersey) Collection.

Page 142 courtesy of the University of
South Carolina.

Page 102 courtesy of the Valentines Museum,
Richmond, VA.

Page 124 courtesy of the
Virginia Historical Society.

Special thanks to the Florida State Archives,
The University of Louisville Photographic
Archives, and the United States Department
of Agriculture Photographic Archives for
their gracious help.